The WORKPLACE BATTLEFIELD

Where great talent
goes to die.

How organizational culture
can make or break your
investment in people.

By

Nick A. Shepherd

ISBN 978-1-7781309-7-7

Cover design by: EduVision Inc.

Author
Nick A. Shepherd
FRSA., FCPA., FCGA., FCCA., FCMC

Dedication

To all the loyal, hardworking people who go to work every day trying to do a good job. Especially to those who slave away in situations where there seem to be all sorts of barriers to trying to get their job done.

To all the managers and leaders out there especially middle managers who sometimes feel like the "meat in the sandwich." Constantly trying to keep employees and everyone else happy and motivated, and at the same time dealing with the demands of senior management.

To senior management and leadership. Sometimes no one understands the challenges of being in charge and having to make tough decisions. But you are not alone. There are people in your organization who want to help.

To everyone. We are all on a journey through life. We all have our own challenges, burdens, issues and concerns. Be kind to one another. Care about trying to build a better world. Our legacy is what we leave behind. Let's make it positive.

Contents

Foreword

When I was appointed President of a mid-sized, private industrial distribution company, the owner and Chairman of the Board gave me some advice. "Nick" he said. "Remember now that you are President, you need to start distancing yourself from the people that you are responsible for. You must do that to remain objective and dispassionate about the decisions that you have to make."

While I felt uncomfortable with the advice, I was keen to make my role a success. It was some of the worst advice that I ever received. For the previous twenty years I had been climbing the corporate ladder, following the finance route. I had become VP Finance of a major computer company and most recently VP Finance of the distribution company where I was now being promoted to President.

During my Journey I became increasingly involved in team building and quality management. Through this I have attended many team development workshops as well as problem solving and process management initiatives. While I clearly had a functional bias, coming from a finance background, it had become clear to me that the human dimensions of the workplace were in fact the more important levers in creating performance effectiveness.

This book draws heavily on my personal experience during those years "in corporate" but also the next thirty years during which I ran my own consulting and professional development company.

The workplace battlefield

While my work started with my bias and background in finance and process management, I was increasingly drawn into the human aspects of organizational performance improvement. I consulted with companies where the people were engaged, enthusiastic and involved in their work and others where the workplace was not a place of passion and performance.

I watched, horror struck, at one team development session at a private family business where the owner berated his wife in front of a group of thirty managers. It seemed that before he felt able to decide for the company, his wife needed to let him know what their plans were for having more children. I never went back there. This was neither effective leadership, nor a good culture and, obviously unacceptable on any level.

I also worked with organizations where tears came to my eyes, as a group of employees from different departments and at different seniority levels, openly shared thoughts, and ideas. They demonstrated a passion for their work. They shared emotions and feelings. They were clearly friends with a shared purpose. Those in leadership positions let others steer the conversation only intervening to help, coach and support when required.

Out of all this experience comes my passion for people. My agreement with Peter Drucker that "culture eats strategy for breakfast every time." My belief is that in spite of people being the hardest aspect of any manager's work, it is the most important. People are fickle, unique, emotional. Yet a well-motivated group of average people can achieve amazing things if they are given the opportunity.

This then is the role of a leader in the 21st century. The knowledge economy. The world where people truly "are the most important asset" – even though they are not an asset and even the phrase or expression can be demeaning. The same as referring to them as "human capital."

The workplace battlefield

This book will show how poor workplace cultures get in the way of people doing amazing things. How hiring the best talent in the world will be a waste of money if leaders fail to create a work environment where people can both be their best and give their best. How a workplace battlefield can destroy all the investment made in both hiring and motivating talented people.

If you want to create a “great place to work” read on.

It is all about culture.

Nick Shepherd
Ottawa, May 2023

1 Introduction

It's no wonder employee engagement globally is so low, at around 30%. This means that 70% of the workforce is disengaged at some level. What a waste of talent.

For many people the idea of going to work is like engaging in a workplace battlefield. Organizations spend astronomical sums of money trying to attract and retain talent, yet have a hard time motivating, engaging, and retaining them. That's because people have to apply their talents through a workplace culture that either supports and accelerates their potential or demeans and destroys it. This is the culture filter that this book addresses.

Is your organization a builder of talent that hires the best and provides a work environment where such talent can be applied and multiplied? Or is the workplace more of a battlefield? Are you in the demolition business of having a culture screen in place that blocks and frustrates the potential of people?

* * * * * * * * * * * * * * * * * * * *

The twenty-first century is often referred to as the age of the fourth industrial revolution. The knowledge economy. The world of intangibles. Everything has changed. Or has it?

Are organizations being run differently? Have things really changed to become human-centric? Is this the age of enlightened leadership and management where "getting the job done" is equally important to making sure that every ounce of talent available is fully engaged?

For most organizations the answer is "no." Media remains full of stories about harassment and inequity in the workplace. Of growing mental health issues – many of which are linked to pressure of work.

Many people, having experienced "life away from the office" during COVID are now resisting pressure to "return to work." Itself a strange phrase almost indicating that managers felt people away from the office weren't working.

We know that action is desperately needed to reduce pollution in major cities. We also know that technology has proven its' ability to allow effective remote work. Yet we seem to be intent on returning to the traditional idea of everyone commuting.

We know that families went through major dislocations during COVID, but they changed habits and routines and made it work. Many people actually "re-discovered" family and the importance of time together. Fathers were able to share the workload of childcare.

Were there some negative experiences where some people used the lack of supervision to spend more time not working? Sure. But in their defense, there is in fact more to life than just work. However, that doesn't take away from the accountability and responsibility that individuals need to embrace.

Some managers, advocates of major return to work initiatives, seem to suggest that unless people are in the office being supervised, productivity will drop, and workers will slacken off.

Interestingly, there are some people that really want to get back to the office. They miss the stimulation, camaraderie and intellectual experience that comes from social interaction with others. They see the opportunity to return to work as a positive move.

There are organizations, particularly in the technology sector but also in other areas, where optional remote working has been available for many years. And it has been working successfully.

Many organizations have stopped using the word "employees" in recognition of the reality that their workforce is now a hybrid of full-time employees, part timers, contract staff and others. These people have all built their own networks and relationships that form the foundation of "getting the job done."

Prior to COVID, many people had already dropped out of the traditional role as an employee, choosing a different lifestyle, and selling their services as freelance consultants, contractors, or agency workers.

Some managers have also changed their approaches to engaging and developing the teams of people that they work with. They have shifted away from seeing people as resources to be planned, organized, controlled, and directed and have focused significantly more attention on developing their leadership skills.

For many this transition has been hard. Many find it impossible. Yet a successful manager works to build relationships with staff that are based on mutual trust, recognition, coaching, support, and development. Through this, people are motivated to become engaged and committed, with a passion for innovation and creativity.

The post COVID world has brought the need for change at work into sharp focus. Organizations who think that the problem is money or financial incentives are often failing to understand the root cause of the problem.

It has long been known that people may use "a better salary" as a reason for leaving – but in reality, people leave relationships not organizations. They leave because they are unengaged and demotivated. Short of recognition and inclusion. Fed up with management making speeches about how important their people are – yet never living up to the promise.

We see the push back even in traditional industries. Major global corporations are having problems in attracting and retaining people. Problems with people trying to "get organized" so that their voice can be heard. Organizations respond by suppressing all efforts to organize yet failing to understand the root cause of the problems.

Too many organizations still don't get it. They are trying to manage people as a generic, holistic mass of human resources. They are using the tools of the 20th century to operate 21st century businesses.

This book is about the emerging challenge of corporate culture and why "its' time has come." Why successful organizations will come to realize that culture is facing the same strategic transition that quality faced in the 1980's. A time when quality had to shift from a functional quality management responsibility to becoming "the way we run the business." A time when strategic approaches to TOTAL quality management evolved. Where quality was built into every aspect of an organization's DNA.

Culture is NOT an HR issue although HR has a significant role to play. Culture is a strategic decision about "how we run the business. How we do things around here." This book looks at the key strategic building blocks required to make a positive, motivating culture become a reality.

2 Post COVID reality

This chapter will expand on how experiencing the two years of COVID shifted the foundations for a critical strategic focus on organizational culture.

Post COVID attitudes to work have changed for many employees and employers. Pre COVID, people would mumble and grumble about work – their boss, co-workers, the tools they have to do the job, the frustrations of commuting. Wasted time spent and trains that were overcrowded and late. Highways that were constantly plugged up with accidents or repairs or just too much traffic. How were organizations responding?

Early adopters – prepared for change.

Before COVID, progressive organizations had already started to think about alternative work patterns. In many industries changes in demographics and availability of staff have already started the move to more flexible workplaces. People could job share, or work from home either occasionally or as a regular part of their routine.

Many organizations had already started changing the way their offices were configured; options such as "hoteling" where shared workspaces were developed so as to reduce overall office space in business sectors where a large proportion of staff were always working off-site – either at client premises or seconded to other organizations.

Information technology has been acquired, implemented and developed so as to allow and support working off-site securely, including transmission and storage of data. Staff had been issued laptop computers loaded with "company only" software; often no data storage was allowed locally, and removable memory was disabled.

With the continued costs and inconvenience of corporate travel, together with the challenge of having the necessary people in the same place at the same time, alternative approaches to meetings have been developed.

Several software based "remote meeting services" had already been established – people were already using Facebook and "face timing" with others. Skype had been introduced initially as an internet-based phone communication but had quickly evolved to video. New services were starting to "hit the market." Organizations also had their own customer-based systems in place.

For these organizations COVID was a significant inconvenience but the shift to a virtual, remote-based workplace was soon possible.

Work climate – prepared for change.

A number of organizations also had workplace climates that were already people centric. Relationships were based on trust. Management continually listened to the "voice of the employee" and opinions and involvement were part of the way the workplace operated.

There were solid relationships established among managers and between managers and all other people. This included suppliers, customers and other third parties. Interactions and relationships were based on collaboration and cooperation for mutual benefit.

Years ago, an author[1] wrote a book on effective managers and talked about developing an "emotional bank account" as a foundation of relationships. Progressive organizations had adopted this concept and worked to build workforce and other relationships founded on effective communications.

Workers in these organizations were always recognized and thanked for a good job. Managers provided counselling, support and coaching when problems occurred. The blame game was avoided with the focus being on continual improvement rather than "the search for the guilty."

Employees' concerns and issues were listened to and acted upon. People who were experiencing personal problems and challenges were helped and supported to work their way through them.

These all contributed deposits to the bank account. Sometimes withdrawals from the account had to take place. A panic workload issue. An extra effort to meet a deadline. A situation where discipline or "corrective action" needed to take place.

A healthy workplace had a positive balance in the emotional bank account and so events were "taken in stride." Others, where no deposits had been made revealed problems, issues, and dissent whenever something special was asked for. There was no trust in place. Employees often felt that they were being taken advantage of and treated unfairly.

Then COVID "hit."

Panic!

Management was forced to shut the workplace down. No one commuted. No one went to work. Manufacturers shut down. Supply

---

[1] Stephen R. Covey, "The 7 Habits of Highly Effective People."

chains shut down. Restaurants and shops shut down. Schools shut down, Nursery and day-care centers shut down. Social services of all types became heavily burdened ***and had to work***.

Organizations and their workforces had to adapt to remote work. Individuals and families developed new ways of working that were organized around the reality of their lifestyle. Many felt they had no choice in the matter, but in most cases made it work.

For those organizations that were already adapting, these changes just sped up what was already happening. Importantly, those organizations that had built collaboration, cooperation, communication and trust into their relationships, were able to shift their working methods quickly. Others were faced with many challenges which, although management was tasked with "managing" the process, the employees were the ones who "had to make it work."

Many people found that the changes they had been forced to make in their lives allowed them to get work done while spending more time with their families and spending less time and money on commuting and family care. Once they adapted, they found there were benefits from not having to "go to work."

People were amazingly resilient. They adapted and made it work. Many "went the extra mile" – in some cases because they had no option but in many cases because of loyalty and commitment to their work and pay cheque. Those who had been in positive, collaborative workplaces were able to quickly adapt and sustain relationships with people they already worked with.

What is important is that in this time period many, many people were left to figure it out for themselves. Innovate. Come up with ideas. Create "work arounds."

Even more importantly, the majority of workers demonstrated that they could work without the boss hanging around. Without being constantly "checked up on." Progressive managers who had built trust with their employees, had confidence that they could "make it work." But there were many who were pessimistic about their ability to supervise and manage their staff without being able to physically see them. They also worried about drops in productivity. They worried that while they had no option but to rely on their staff, they felt personally exposed and at risk.

While individual results varied, there was little drop in production and people got their work done. There were situations where people were found to be not working, and this created calls for direct supervision – even putting cameras on peoples' computers to check they "were working" when they claimed they were. Not much trust being shown here!

The world went on – and we survived.

In many cases people went "over and above" in terms of making these new arrangements work. Good managers continued with their effective communications, engagement, and trust, while others may have started to realize "hey, this might even work." Then there were those who couldn't wait to have their people back at the office where they could start "managing again."

Meanwhile, many employees were showered with thanks and gratitude for making it work. In particular, people like health care workers came through as true professionals. Putting themselves at risk and caring for others. Working incredibly long hours. Trying to make do with shortages of supplies because supply chains were severely disrupted and because suddenly demand for certain items globally had soared.

There had been a major learning opportunity and people had risen to the occasion. More important still, they compared their current arrangements – which in their own minds were working – the job was getting done, with the way things were before COVID.

Working at home they had autonomy and, in many cases, had much more control over their workload. They were able to manage their time to suit their own schedule and as long as the work was done, how it was done, and what hours were worked wasn't important. They were able to focus on the task at hand. Fewer office politics and harassment. No interruptions because the boss calls a sudden "spur of the minute meeting."

No getting up and getting out early to catch the commuter train with all the hassle. No arriving at work already frazzled by the experience. People recognized that "the way things were before" wasn't so great. There was a better way.

So – let's all go back to work now.

Wow – not so fast.

Even though the choice might not have been theirs to make, the lifestyle changes meant many people were reluctant and unwilling to just go back to how things were. They now knew that an alternative not only existed but had been proven to work.

Plans for returning to work were vastly varied. In many situations employees were never even consulted - organizations dictated terms for coming back to work, only to find they were so unpopular or unworkable that they had to rethink their whole approach.

International organizations had major issues. Different rules applied in different countries – and even different by state and province. People trying to figure out whether they had to go back or not, and what levels of flexibility or options they had were faced with all sorts of different rules.

After some people had returned to work and had the opportunity to reconnect socially with their work colleagues, it didn't take long for the old problems, issues, and resentments to rear their head. People were now no longer willing to accept behaviors or circumstances that they knew could be improved. Inequity, unfairness, unreasonable working conditions plus the frustrations of commuting all started to create the "perfect storm."

Management started to struggle. Many organizations had focused on ways to save money when business "crashed" and some had let leases lapse, downsized to smaller or even closed some offices. The work team and the work itself might have remained the same, but the changes to facilities meant that the work environment had changed. Some people were expected to change locations.

Some people returned to work to find the workspace completely disrupted. There was no office space or even desks for some. People sat on the floor with their laptops having ZOOM meetings with others – some at the office, and some still at home or in other locations.

The "great resignation" that had started with a trickle during the pandemic now started to gain momentum. "Enough" people said. And they walked – either to another job, as demand was increasing, or even out of the workforce for a time.

Growing dissent

Many of those who returned to work soon started to wonder why things hadn't changed. Why they couldn't have more flexibility. Some organizations successfully implemented a four-day week that was received positively – and with no loss in productivity. So, changes were possible.

Many workers, especially those in the health care sector returned to work feeling good about the success of their efforts in helping people survive COVID. They had felt the appreciation of the general public. Yet many were faced with staffing issues coupled with a major backlog in other medical activities such as cancer treatments and other surgical operations. The pressure continued – but many soon felt that in spite of all their efforts, nothing had improved. In fact, because of many funding issues even less resources were available.

Then – as the global supply chains adjusted and the effects of the war in Ukraine started to take effect especially in the energy sector, inflation started to increase. Not only were working conditions a challenge, but now money was even shorter. In the UK, nurses and doctors were joined by railway workers, government workers and many others in strike action. Elsewhere there was anxiety and disruption.

In parallel to this, organizations were investigating the concept of employee engagement. The solution was obviously to try and improve employee engagement and possibly offer more money to attract new hires. Some organizations – short of staff, decided to do away with the interview process and hire whoever came along with minimum screening.

The Post Covid world is a new world. While many old issues in the workplace continue, they have now become more visible, and people are more prepared to voice their opinion and even walk away from jobs.

The problem is that many people in management just don't get it. Some are resorting to more authoritarian management styles. Forcing people to fit their business model. This is making matters worse.

The real underlying problem is that a screen exists in every organization that acts like a filter. This is the culture screen. This is what is increasingly blocking operational effectiveness and causing frustration.

Culture is now a strategic imperative and those who fail to understand the causes and fix the issues will continue to lose staff, have trouble hiring and suffer from a continuing lack of commitment, innovation and creativity combined with poor productivity.

Part 1

The Culture Screen

Understanding how
people's talent
can be blocked.

3 The Culture screen.

> Every organisation has a culture screen. A clean screen acts like a clean filter and allows the unimpeded flow of talent. A dirty or blocked screen slows it down or stops it. Organizations can hire the best talent in the world, but it won't matter.

A recent post on Facebook told of a story of a healthcare worker who had two jobs. One, where she loved to go to work. The other, she just did her job, collected her pay cheque and went home. Why the difference? The culture screen.

One work environment was aligned and managed so as to create a positive workplace – a clean filter. One where there were almost no barriers to getting her job done and where she was appreciated as true talent and valued as a person. The other essentially had a dirty filter. Blocked with all sorts of impediments to her ability to get her job done. She was treated as part of the organization's human resources – much like the other resources that management acquires and pays for.

There is a direct link between the work environment and employee engagement (not to be confused with employee satisfaction). The latter can exist without engagement being present. In fact, in the second example above, she may have responded as being "somewhat satisfied." She was paid at or above the market rate for her job. Given work that she could do and received clear instructions. At the end of her shift, she went home. She did what she was paid for *but no more.*

The difference is that satisfaction contains no passion. No driving force that encourages her to be "all that she can be." To go that extra mile when needed. To fix her own problems rather than stopping work and asking someone else to do it because "that's not her job."

Let's not confuse this with unions and collective agreements. If management was engaging with people and making them true partners in the business, many of the drivers for unionization would disappear. Uninvolved, disenchanted and unfairly treated people want representation. If management doesn't provide it someone else will.

The culture screen.

The idea is quite simple. You pour resources in the top. The better the flow, the more productive and creative the business model.

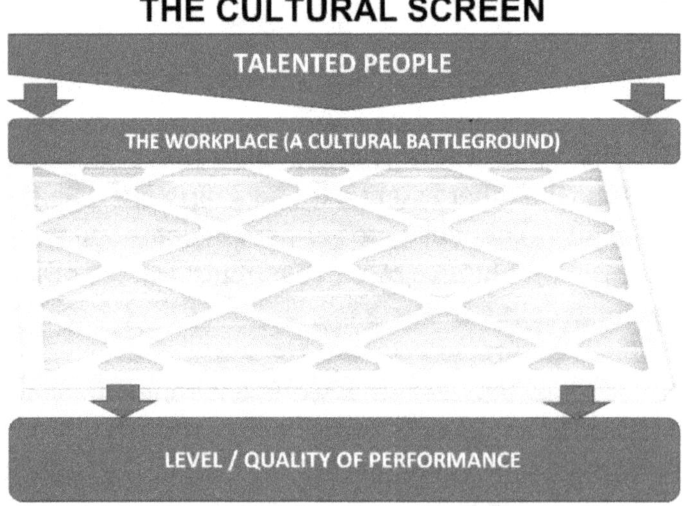

While the picture focuses on the input of talented people, the level of blockage works in a similar way on all "resources."

As an example:

- Poor relationships with suppliers and customers.
- Poor, out-of-date tools and equipment.
- Poor equipment that frequently fails.

The link to performance is clear. The more effectively inputs are converted to outputs and outcomes, the better performance will be. On a "system level" this is reflected in better quality, on time performance, higher productivity, and usually enhanced profitability. Profitability is better because most resources cost money. The more effectively the resources are utilized, the lower the cost per unit of output.

Given the importance of environmental and climate change issues, these also benefit. In many cases there are no "costs involved" per se, so these are referred to as "externalities" - someone else pays. But the impact on society – as someone else usually pays, (as an example, the taxpayers in the community), is less negative.

For the human inputs the effect is massive. For many organizations their payroll, benefits and other "human related" costs are their biggest expense. Enhancing the conversion of human input to output can therefore have the greatest effect.

BUT...

Don't ask the accountants what the cost of poor productivity actually is. Especially when it relates to the ***lost opportunity of human potential.***

Most "people related" costs are added together in financial statements so there is little idea of what the "hidden waste from poor culture" is.

The only guide that there may be, is the total level of "system" performance – which is usually profitability. But knowing this financial outcome, may hide other, less positive outcomes. Staff stress and turnover and others.

Not to say human performance cannot be measured. In manufacturing they have done it for years – but it usually measures actual PHYSICAL output compared to plan. In the knowledge world, how can one measure actual intellectual / value adding performance versus potential? Much harder. (That's why people are now trying to measure "employee engagement" – which we will come back to later).

So, what are the things that get in the way of human talent and block up the culture screen. Let's take another look.

THE CULTURAL SCREEN

TALENTED PEOPLE

THE WORKPLACE (A CULTURAL BATTLEGROUND)

Excess bureaucracy
Poor systems, tools and equipment
Misaligned policies and procedures
Poor management / leadership
Failure to integrate
Irresponsible / anti-social behavior

LEVEL / QUALITY OF PERFORMANCE
Engagement, motivation, retention, innovation, creativity, agility, change...

The workplace battlefield

It's called a "cultural battleground" because for many people that's EXECTLY what their workplace feels like. Everything that needs to be done is like fighting a battle.

Organizations spend major amounts of money in developing talent strategies. Selecting staff and investing in "on boarding" and other activities. They "pour people into the top of their business model."

But when these talented people arrive in the workplace and try to contribute their skills, knowledge, experience, and other talents they find barriers. These are the barriers of a poor culture. Many people soon become de-motivated and often leave.

The result is not only lower productivity – because as one would imagine things take longer to get done – but it's also the cause of stress and mental sickness for many people. It also drives a lack of employee engagement, demotivation, lower retention and higher turnover, lower innovation and creativity, less agility and – if not resistance to change, as a minimum a harder change management process.

A culture screen that fails to facilitate work effectiveness is an unsafe and unhealthy workplace.

There are six major factors shown in the diagram. You may know more – but here is the idea. ALL of these factors are inter-dependent so collectively they operate as the "work climate." When people talk about culture – this is it. This is "the way things get done around here." What are the six major categories? (They are not in any order of importance and as stated are all interrelated).

- **Excess bureaucracy**. Typically, the way things are set up to work, especially considering controls and risk management.
- **Poor systems, tools, and equipment**. The essence of a business model is providing people with "the tools" they need to do the job.

- **Misaligned policies and procedures**. Defined ways of working that are inconsistent with an organization's values, goals and objectives.
- **Poor management and leadership**. Either poor management of task or ineffective "enabling" of work relationships.
- **Failure to integrate**. The organization fails to work as a holistic, smoothly functioning system.
- **Irresponsible or anti-social behavior**. People are treated "badly," and decision making is poor and inconsistent.

Any one or combination of these factors will work as a blocker to overall effective operations.

When organizations talk about problems with a poor culture, they often discuss outcomes of the culture. Things such as:

- Higher turnover, loss of key staff
- Inconsistency
- Unethical decision making
- Poor communication
- Lack of trust
- People playing the "blame game."
- Unfairness
- Harassment, bullying
- Not inclusive; diversity seen as negative.

Many of these are outcomes of a poor culture that collectively leads to lower productivity. People are often resilient and will "put up with it." But they will never be the best that they can be. The leaders' job is to create a positive culture where these problems are eliminated. Where a toxic culture cannot take hold.

The next chapters outline and discuss each of the items shown as barriers to talent in the culture screen.

4 Bureaucracy

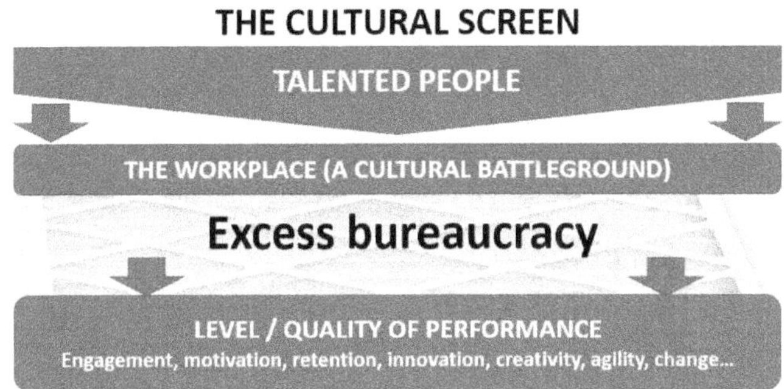

Issue

Levels of administration, supervision, oversight, and control seem to get in the way of getting the job done. This may start at the governance level where excessive concern over risk goes too far and stifles innovation and creativity.

Bureaucracy can be designed in, but it can also creep in without warning. Overly complex rules and policies. Overzealous "control" concerns. Lack of delegation or trust. Bias towards cost control which inhibits people's ability to act. Many events, issues and occurrences block the culture screen.

Action

Be constantly aware of the balance between risk management and innovation and creativity. Enhance approaches to building trust through better hiring and development of all people. Empower managers to question and remove blockages to performance. Ask people "what gets in the way of you being innovative and creative at work?" Ask those with governance responsibility "are we sure that the controls we have in place are necessary and are not impeding the work of the talent we have available?"

Discussion

Bureaucracy may be an intentional part of the culture, and may be "designed in." This would be the case in the way that many government organizations are structured. They exhibit the classical elements of a designed bureaucratic system[2]:

- procedural regularity,
- a hierarchical system of accountability and responsibility,
- specialization of function,
- designed for continuity,
- a legal-rational basis, and
- fundamental conservatism.

Governments have this for good reasons. Politics change but the underlying public service needs a level of stability. However, in looking at the culture screen, we are more concerned about where bureaucracy gets in the way of an organization's strategic direction. This is where an organization "becomes overly concerned with procedure at the expense of efficiency or common sense." Think about it this way.

- **Strategic bureaucracy**: designed to meet the organization's needs specifically related to risk and continuity.
- **Creeping bureaucracy**: caused where an organization brings in more controls as it grows to "protect its interests."
- **Acquired bureaucracy**: where a merger occurs between two organizations, and one gradually destroys the other.

---

[2] Encyclopedia Britannica

The workplace battlefield

Why is it that even using the word strikes fear into the minds of innovators and entrepreneurs?

One way of thinking about bureaucracy is its' relationship to risk management. Typically, the more risk adverse an organization is (like the civil service) the more bureaucracy is required to control risk.

Typically, this means a host of policies, procedures, approvals, limited delegation of authority, everything must be reviewed and approved etc. etc. Innovative and creative people often find it frustrating to work in a "high control" environment. How do you avoid falling into the trap of creating blockages caused by this?

- Realize that cultures are unique to the organization involved.
- The people hired must be those who can successfully work within this type of environment.
- Mergers and acquisitions between high risk and low risk organizations are not likely to deliver the desired results or may fail.
- If a business is created to innovate and take risks, don't kill this culture by bringing in excessive controls. It kills the culture.
- Processes must be "engineered" to optimize the combination of risk management and optimum outputs and outcomes (performance).
- Don't try and combine or integrate a high risk / high control organization with a low risk / lower control organization.

While the last point applies to mergers and acquisitions it also applies to efforts to apply "economies of scale" to organizations. Often trying to share areas like support services can create problems. These "partners" are often difficult to deal with. Here are some simple examples that "don't mix:"

- A Michelin star restaurant is rarely in the fast-food business.
- Precision electronics are not assembled in a dusty, cheap warehouse space.
- Nuclear grade tubing is not manufactured alongside budget price plumbing pipes.
- You would likely not take a Ferrari to be serviced at a corner garage.

In building a business model, with en effective workplace climate and culture, there is a constant balance and tradeoff between managing risk and optimizing performance.

Managing this balance is often a "tug of war" between those wanting more safeguards and controls such as accounting, and legal and those looking for less control such as design / development, operations, and sales.

Neither is right or wrong – the key is the correct STRATEGIC balance.

As business evolves and changes, a board and leadership team must always monitor the balance between the two extremes. In a way the ideal point is to be "just in control." Maximizing potential to take reasonable and planned risk within a defined tolerance for problems being allowed to occur.

Anyone working within a particular type of organization must be able to operate as effectively as possible. They must not be placed in the position of having controls imposed upon them that get in the way of doing the work but have limited perceived benefit. An example.

> *Many organizations put expense controls in place that require certain levels of authorization. A highly skilled maintenance mechanic, who has the responsibility of supporting and maintaining a highly expensive piece of capital equipment is not allowed to purchase low value parts required to keep the equipment running effectively.*

Does that make operational sense? She is accountable to keep the equipment running effectively yet is constantly frustrated by having barriers put in her way, waiting for people, who often know nothing about the equipment, to sign off on the purchase. Frustrating? Non-productive?

Be on the lookout for creeping bureaucracy

So often – especially where culture is not being managed strategically, an organization known for innovation and creativity starts to get slowed down. Why?

- **Growth**. As innovative leaders and entrepreneurs scale their organizations and start to bring in more levels of management including specialists in finance and other areas, controls start to be implemented that may slowly change the risk profile.
- **Maturity**. Similar to the above, as a business matures market prices and operating margins often decline. This requires "more control" to be instituted. This desire to protect the business often kills the innovation that created it in the first place.
- **Downturns**. When an economy tightens, management – especially this who have a bias for "command and control" tend to implement added controls and also reduce headcount. This creates the perfect storm of less people to do the work but more difficulty in getting it

done. (The outcome will often be demotivated staff who hang around because the economy is tight but as soon as it turns around, look for another job).

This is why culture is not a passive issue, but one that requires strategic focus. Business is always evolving and changing which means the "way we do things around here" must be managed – including the levels of controls.

Be on the lookout for acquired bureaucracy

The seed of this problem can occur with a merger or acquisition. Consider the many drivers behind strategic M&A's such as:

- An organization seeking to "change," looks to acquire another that has the skills and capabilities it needs.
- An organization that has fallen behind in technology acquires another to provide the skills and capabilities needed.
- An organization seeking territorial expansion seeks to acquire one already operating within a certain region.
- A group wishing to growth, seeks to acquire a portfolio of small, privately owned, and managed companies and build a "group."
- A business seeks to franchise by attracting private business owners to merge and become part of the group.

Are the two organizations compatible in control and culture? These transactions are happening all the time. The success is not great. KPMG state on their M&A website that around 69% of deals (buying and selling of a business) fail to achieve their deal objective and deliver on long-term shareholder value. Many studies – especially more recent ones include "clashes of culture" as a problem area. Some notable examples are:

- Amazon and Whole Foods (2017) $13.7 billion

- AT&T and Time Warner (2018) $85 billion
- AT&T and Direct TV (2015) $49 billion
- Google and Motorola (2012): US$12.5 billion.
- America Online and Time Warner (2001): US$65 billion.
- Daimler-Benz and Chrysler (1998): US$36 billion.

In researching all these situations, at some point the issue of trying to integrate different cultures was mentioned. In most cases the merger resulted in major financial losses for the organization.

There are also examples of franchise relationship problems where efforts to enhance the franchisor profitability are having negative effects on the critical relationships with franchises.

- McDonalds, 2020 dispute on increasing fees charged. $68 million reduced to $26 million after independent review. (Whole package as initially proposed in 2020, was $170 million).
- Time Hortons / Restaurant Brands International. In 2017, a group of Canadian Tim Horton's franchisees formed an association to combat "mismanagement" of the brand since its sale to Restaurant Brands International in 2014.

Very often the franchisee is a large corporate entity, whereas the franchisor is a smaller, entrepreneurial unit. One of THE most critical issues in mergers and acquisitions is dealing with "the way each company does things around here" – i.e., the culture. The impact of attitudes towards risk management and control, and the level of bureaucracy are critical culture issues that must be strategically managed.

Ineffective and unnecessary levels of control will create blockages in the culture screen. While managing this is always a balancing act, most organizations need to be "just in control." For innovation and creativity to occur some risk must be taken. If highly talented people are brought into a work environment where there are excessive levels of bureaucracy, they will quickly become de-motivated, and disengaged. They will not apply innovation and creativity. Their talents will be under-utilized. And they probably won't be around for long.

INTERNAL CONTROL

Bureaucracy often occurs when governance systems are no longer "fit for purpose." There are two aspects where a critical shift has occurred and must be reflected.

First, competition has heightened the potential for individuals and organizations to cut corners, potentially either risking breaking the law or acting unethically (with or without management's knowledge). This, combined with the challenges of managing international operations where the workplace is often composed of people with many different experiences and backgrounds, makes "control based on behavior" a growing imperative.

Second – traditional structural controls built into processes, systems, and procedures are becoming less capable of stopping problems. Organizations have often stepped up their systems of internal control to try and stop these problems occurring. But innovative, creative people will always find ways to "work around" a system that gets in the way.

To exert control, organizations today must move from a bias towards process-based controls towards one that also sees control as a core factor in desired behaviour.

Traditional controls – especially under "command and control" leadership have been based on a "low consultative" basis. A more consultative based approach that ensures are balanced and "don't unnecessarily get in the way of the task being performed" is required.

This is not about abrogating the need for control in an effort to create greater flexibility. It is an approach that more effectively balances managing risk with sustaining competitiveness. It can be referred to as collaborative control. The following chart shows the four segments that are control and collaboration driven.

Q1 demonstrates a traditional approach to controls where consultation and engagement is low, and controls are imposed based on a top-down assessment of risk. This is a potential blocker to talent, innovation, and creativity.

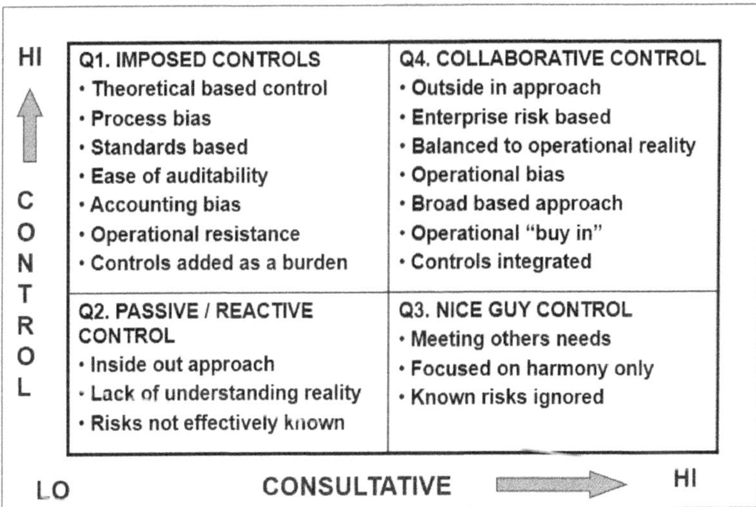

Q2 reflects low engagement but also a lack of risk awareness. This is the top down "laizzez-faire" approach (which is usually a disaster waiting to happen).

Controls in a people-centric based work environment must come from a higher level of engagement. Where input from the people doing the work is gathered and balanced with the need for effective oversight and control.

Q3 reflects a desire to become more consultative, but without an understanding of the reality of risk. This often happens where the bias swings towards "just allow people to do what they want" because of a fear of stifling creativity. (New start-up technology businesses often have a high consultative low control approach initially. Sadly, this is also a disaster waiting to happen, and when control becomes an issue, they often revert to Q1).

Q4 reflects where we want to be. Solid understanding and knowledge of the need for control coupled with a consultative mindset that understands the need to minimize barriers to getting the job done.

The evolution of internal control systems can become a major cause of bureaucracy in the culture screen and block the efforts of talented people just trying to get the job done.

5 Poor systems, tools, and equipment

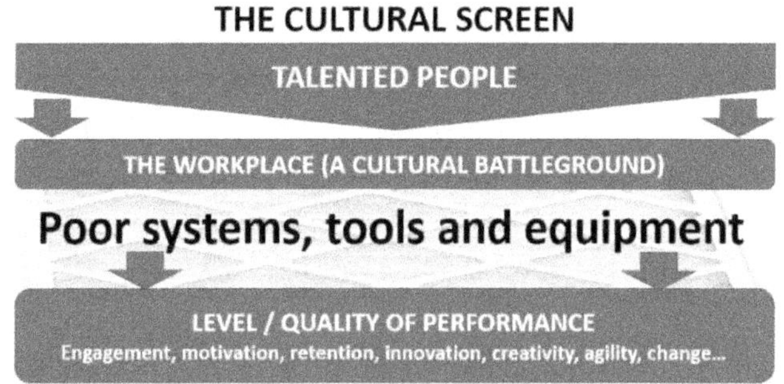

Issue

When people arrive in the workplace they are "integrated" with the resources they need to get the job done. This can be computer systems or any other tools and equipment (and other people, that we discuss later relative to personal behavior and the building of effective relationships).

Many management systems do a good job of reporting down-time of equipment, but few do a good job of intellectual downtime. It is hard to measure the ROI of providing the necessary tools and equipment if one doesn't know the cost of NOT having these available.

If the provision of these resources are not positive enablers, not only will productivity suffer but so will morale. If nothing is done to fix the problem people will become disengaged and frustrated. Inadequate tools and equipment will become a blocker in the culture screen.

Action

Recognize that human talent is a key part of an overall system; the engagement and performance of talent can only work well in conjunction with other parts of the system. (Basic theory of constraints thinking).

When developing position descriptions ensure that a specification is developed defining the fully functioning support equipment that an individual requires to perform their work.

Listen to, and support people who identify blockages related to inadequate systems, tools and equipment – and support from other areas. These are not troublemakers but "canaries in the coal mine" of engagement problems that block a culture screen.

Discussion

A survey included in a management book "First, Break the Rules" has, as a key question "do I have the tools and equipment necessary for me to do my job?" This is a foundational factor in the culture screen – especially for people in organizations where technology is at the heart of the business.

The tools and equipment to do the job are what might be called "the nuts and bolts."

What is needed will vary depending on the type of organization and the job involved. Not having the required tools and equipment causes frustration.

The sorts of problems and issues that people face is often the result of budget allocation of scarce funding. It is often hard to know where this is occurring. Equipment down time can be tracked and monitored but intellectual downtime is more challenging. People may moan and complain but are often required to "make do" with what is provided. This causes frustration. Examples can include:

- Using outdated software. (e.g., ineffective meeting scheduling and management).
- Poor system design / user interface (e.g., having to repeat data entry, poor validation approaches for problem prevention).
- Out of date / unlicensed software versions.
- Problems with the slow network response time.
- Not having the equipment close to where it is needed.
- Software changes made without consultation / communication.
- Lack of safety equipment.
- Using poorly maintained equipment.
- Inadequate availability of supplies.
- Poor filing systems (both paper and data).
- Frequent breakdowns due to poor / no preventative maintenance
- Inadequate support staff to help with problem solving.
- Poor office ergonomics / damaged equipment.

The list could go on. It's often the little things that happen that are frustrating, and which can accumulate over time. So many of these issues occur when the people doing the work are not consulted in the acquisition, design, or development stages; nor are they often asked, "how's it working?"

In many situations individuals may try and escalate the problems to their immediate supervisor, but due to workload, inter-departmental disputes, or personality problems, even the managers may be frustrated. They may feel they are powerless to "enable" their staff to do the required work and just "brush off" the problem as they know there is nothing that they can do about it.

Not only will these problems contribute to poor culture, but they are also hidden causes of poor productivity. It's what is going on "below the surface" that management is often not aware of.

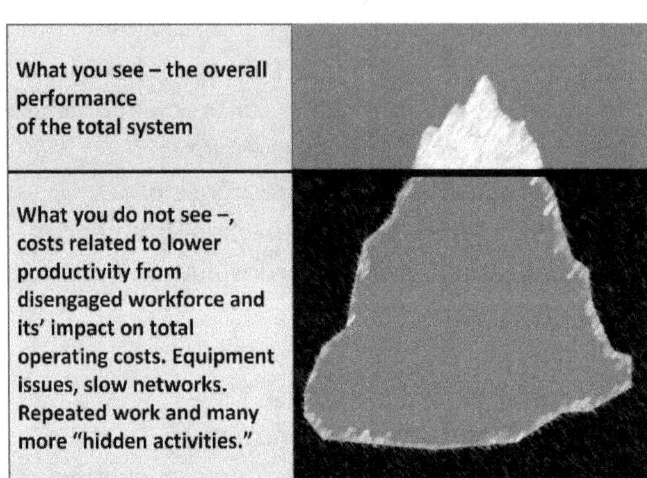

This type of hidden culture problem is described in much more detail in the book "The Cost of Poor Culture." The hidden cost is considerable.

As in many culture screen blockages, having the necessary tools and equipment overlaps with other areas.

An important role of effective leaders and managers is ensuring that the people who work for them have what is needed. Very often they are dependent upon other departments to provide this. As an example, the IT department will play a critical role in almost every organization today. Information technology has become almost fully integrated into almost every job.

When an employee raises a problem with their manager, how empowered is the manager to be able to fix it? How well does inter-departmental communications work? How high a priority is getting an issue that is blocking productivity treated versus working on a new system? Is IT working with the same strategic values and priorities as every other department?

So often organizational structures are the cause of breakdowns and blockages in the culture screen. This is why "lack of integration" is cited as another key category.

Often the financial planning processes are also dysfunctional. Decisions are made to "make the numbers come out right" and financial budgets become disconnected from the operational budgets of different departments. Departments develop their plans for the upcoming period based on certain assumptions that are built into its financial plan. If the financial part of the plan is arbitrarily changed so that expenses are reduced to meet profit projections – operational plans are impacted. If these are not reworked, then there is a major disconnect.

Often managers are told "to do your best" when this happens, or "you need to figure out how to make it happen." While setting aggressive goals and tasks will always be important, if it creates a situation where people are unable to do their job and become de-motivated – that's a problem.

The impact of IT on employees

As IT becomes more pervasive it is interesting to assess the impact that its' effectiveness has on employee satisfaction and performance. A recent (2022) report by Freshworks[3] found a number of key issues:

91%, or 9 out of 10 employees reported that they're frustrated with their work software,
71% of leaders acknowledge that employees will consider looking for a new job if their current employer does not provide access to the tools, technology, or information they need to do their jobs well.

[3] Freshworks "The State of Workplace Technology." 2022

Significant workplace failures on technology people use every day. Slow speeds (51%), extended IT response times (34%), lack of collaboration between departments (30%), missing important features/capabilities (28%) and lack of automation (25%).

Commenting on this report, the blog Venture Beat[4] stated that *"Insufficient technology doesn't just harm the employee experience – it's also harming the wider business. Throughout the pandemic, businesses spent an estimated $15 billion extra per week on technology to enable remote working, according to KPMG. Freshworks' survey reveals that dated tech is restricting business productivity, as frustrated employees grapple with daily IT challenges. More than half (57%) of unsatisfied employees say their current software makes them less productive. Nearly half (44%) of employees surveyed say the time spent dealing with technology issues has increased since the beginning of the pandemic."* The blog goes on to add,

"…and employee stress levels are soaring due to limiting technology – nearly half (49%) of employees surveyed report that inadequate workplace technology causes them to feel stressed and 48% claim it has negatively impacted their mental health. Business leaders agree, with 38% reporting that their failure to deliver adequate workplace technology to their stakeholders causes them to feel stressed."

Note that this report was created in 2022, which is almost **20 years** after the book "First break all the rules" identified that a major cause of low employee engagement was "not having the tools and equipment necessary to do my job." No wonder employee engagement remains at such low levels.

IT budgets consume an increasing amount of corporate expenditure. Is value for money being generated in terms of an effective culture?

---

4 https://venturebeat.com/enterprise-analytics/report-91-of-employees-say-theyre-frustrated-with-workplace-tech/ extracted 23rd April 2023

Other tools and equipment

Everything costs money and as a result the longer things can be made to last, the better it will be financially. While gross measures of performance and productivity can be developed it is hard to determine the underlying "failure costs" that are being incurred because of lost productivity at the individual level. (Unless people are asked, listened to, heard and their input acted upon!).

Providing people with up-to-date tools and equipment is a constant "balancing act" to remain competitive. Financial pressures will often work to try and extend the life of equipment. Users will often look for the most recent versions of equipment that they are required to use. The more people are engaged and involved in managing this "balancing act" the less negative impact they will have as a blocker on the culture screen.

Trying to reduce maintenance costs can also be a problem. The older equipment becomes, the greater the challenge of sustaining its operation. So, it's not just the equipment that can have an impact on the individual, it is the effectiveness of the support framework that ensures continued operations.

This is another area where overlaps occur between culture screen blockers. Sometimes, support staff may want to fix the problems but are slowed down or held back from obtaining what they need to do the work by policies and procedures. These may have been developed by legal or accounting, that focus more on "control" than on responding quickly to the operational need of employees. (Back to bureaucracy again).

World class organizations often "upend" traditional relationships in support functions. Some measure the effectiveness of support based on its responsiveness to operational issues, rather than purely cost control and up-time. One example is the way that maintenance works in Toyota facilities.

The problem is not limited to equipment but can include the materials and supplies that people need. Both their adequacy and availability.

Leadership needs to ***knock down all the barriers*** that people identify that contribute to a "less then effective" work environment. Unless this people-centric focus is systemic, there will be culture screen blockers.

People costs are the highest expenditure for most organizations. Having a culture screen that blocks this talent from working at its optimum level of effectiveness is a major driver of disengagement, demotivation and ultimately loss of staff.

6 Misaligned policies and procedures

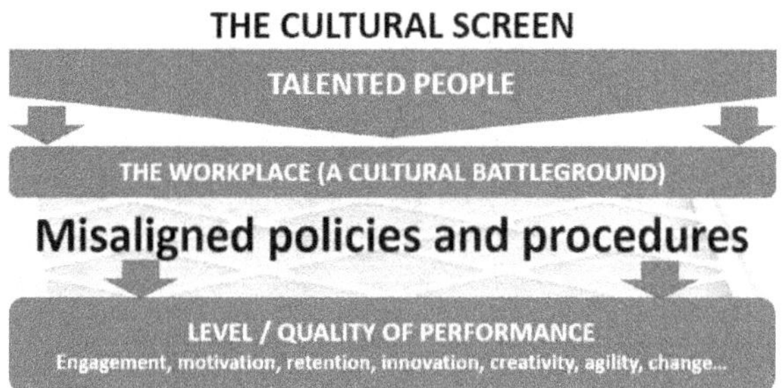

Issue

All employees are required to follow policies and procedures. But when these get in the way (see discussion on bureaucracy) or they are out of alignment with what management speaks about, then they can be a problem.

Organizational values, that should underpin behavior, talk about how we do things around here and what we believe in. Most organizations never carry out an "alignment check" between messages related to high level statements, commitment, and beliefs, and the policies and procedures people are expected to follow. This misalignment is the source of disengagement, blockages in the culture screen, and loss in performance.

Action

Use organizational behavioral values as a foundation for developing policies and procedures. Perform a reality check that seeks to evaluate each policy and procedure against the stated beliefs and values of the organization. Bring these into alignment.

Engage with staff who can point out areas where "what we say and what we do" are out of alignment. Ask them, "What do we tell you to do, that in reality is inconsistent with what you believe we actually want to see?"

Discussion

One of the greatest frustration that staff face is often a misalignment between statements that talk about what an organization believes in and the policies and procedures that they are required to follow. This is similar to problems with systems, tools, and equipment. Let's use some examples.

- Organizations that state that their suppliers "are part of the team" yet ignore contractual terms and conditions and always pay their suppliers late.
- Statements about "...our valued customers..." yet but when a customer tries to solve a problem is told by the service agent "...I'm sorry about it and agree with you but unfortunately that is our policy."
- Organizations who state they are customer focused yet create challenges for customers through ineffective automated call systems, call centers that suffer from a lack of knowledgeable staff, and significant wait times. (Especially those with a recorded message that says "...your call is important to us so please stay on the line." (Many of these strategies purely driven by cost).
- Organizations that state that bringing in "new talent" is a critically important activity but defer orientation training because of budget constraints.

On one occasion during a break in an executive (C Suite) team session, there was a conversation that went something like this:

VP European marketing to CEO. "Can we do something about our travel policy? I recently wanted to take the train but was told I had to fly as it was the cheapest option. Taking the train seemed the right thing to do to me. I would have had much more time to work. There would have been less time wasted at the airport for security and everything else and its' more environmentally sensitive."

CEO. "Makes sense to me. What was the cost difference?"

VP European Marketing. "Less than a hundred euros. But I was told by finance that if they ignored the rules for me, they would have to do it for everyone. When I pointed out that I would have more time for work, they told me that this wasn't part of the cost justification, because it's not reported or measured."

CEO. "That raises an interesting challenge. I know we talk about work-life balance being important. We also talk about being committed to reducing carbon emissions and climate change, yet we seem to have a policy that suggests we do the opposite, and that financial cost is the only consideration. We need to figure out how to fix that because it doesn't make sense."

I wonder if they ever fixed it, or did it remain a frustrater?

We discussed another example in chapter four in bureaucracy. The example of a maintenance mechanic having to follow procedures driven by financial risk and control; it appeared to ignore any other statements that may have been made by the company about "placing trust in the people" and "our respected, valued and talented workforce."

Another example is around the decision-making process. Many organizations have strict controls relating to the justification of purchasing equipment. Often these controls and approaches to justification are heavily weighted to financial returns. As an example, during a conversation with a Board of Directors, the following dialogue took place during a discussion about "what the company's stated values meant in practice."

The company had stated that it was committed to "being environmentally responsible." One director was asked *"how do you interpret this?"* He proceeded to explain that wherever the company worked, there were legal requirements for the environment that had to be met, and that being responsible was following those laws and regulations."

Another director responded that he totally disagreed with that interpretation. He explained *"we have developed, and we know of the best operating practices because we have facilities in some of the most highly regulated operations particularly in Europe. Are you telling me that if we operate somewhere else that allows us to get away with lower requirements, that we would only do the minimum necessary?"*

The other director agreed that was exactly what he meant. The company should only do what it is legally obligated to do. There followed a heated debate about what a simple statement like "being environmentally responsible actually meant in practice." This was a great example of a legal / financial / compliance driven approach to decision making versus a values / culture-based approach.

Having stated that they want to be environmentally responsible, if the company then made purchase decisions purely on legal and financial terms, how would that be interpreted by the employees? Especially when many would consider this decision "doing the minimum necessary" – even if it is meeting legal requirements? It would certainly raise some concerns about the integrity of management – especially if it was also in a workplace where the company had stated that it was committed to acting ethically.

This is why work practices that employees operate within on a day-to-day basis MUST be aligned with statements related to behavior. Policies and procedures become "the way we do things around here" – and if these are not reconciled with any statements related to expectations of behavior, then the culture will evolve rather than be managed and will reflect what past practices have been.

If an organization then comes out with some high-level statements about "corporate values" as guidance for expected behavior – but never checks these against policies or procedures, then there is likely to be frustration. This leads to a lack of trust and a skeptical attitude towards what management says versus what is actually done.

Is your desired culture determining your policies and procedures? Or are your policies and procedures defining your culture?

Is culture being strategically managed?

The larger an organization becomes, the greater this challenge. While senior leaders may be committed to all their statements about the environment, culture, "people are our most important asset" etc., many of them have little connection with the reality of day-to-day operations "at the front line." Trying to solve this by becoming an "undercover boss" may be helpful but it's not changing the culture. It may even be interpreted as being dishonest.

Remote work and "the great resignation"

One major policy that is creating increasing problems is the issue of remote work. A large portion of the global workforce experienced two years of major disruption during COVID. Many made significant personal changes to allow businesses to continue to operate, by re-arranging their lives. This experience showed that:

- People went to great lengths to help their employers continue to operate.
- Employers worked in partnership with staff, so that both could "survive" in the reality of a world where people could not "go to the office."
- Technology proved capable of enabling remote work in a seamless and productive manner.
- People realized the impact that commuting to work had on their lifestyle, stress, and productivity.
- The majority of people, when allowed flexibility in how they managed their work, acted responsibly.
- When people were faced with a "return to work," many pushed back, knowing that the "old way" really wasn't necessary anymore.
- Saving money on commuting costs, many were actually financially better off (it was like a pay raise).

This disruption also reinforced to many employees the importance and value of the workplace as a social environment. Many missed the collaborative and supportive work environment.

These people typically already worked in a workplace culture where "the culture screen was clean." Their skills and talents were recognized, and an environment existed for collaboration, innovation, and creativity. Many of these people actually wanted to return to work.

However, the impact of the daily commute on both the individuals as well as the increasingly important climate impact was seen by many employees as an opportunity to re-think the way their work was being undertaken. Maybe a full return to the office was not necessary? Maybe a hybrid system combining days at the office with time at home? Maybe a reduction in the work week?

For other employees, who had been operating in a less effective workplace culture, there was the opposite reaction. They realized how the stress and problems of being in the workplace, in an environment where the "culture screen was blocked" was NOT something they wanted to return to. They had realized they were quite capable of doing their work either fully remotely or with only a reduced portion of time at the office.

Everybody came out of COVID with a new appreciation of how their work life impacted their personal health and wellness. Plus, they knew change was possible. A new way could be made to work.

Progressive management realized the impact of these experiences and have been working with their employees to develop mutually acceptable alternatives.

Less progressive management, who had been continually concerned about people "not working hard" when they were working remotely, or "not being at their desk" when required reacted differently.

Some organizations saw the return to work as a way of re-establishing control over the workforce. (Not to say that some organizations DID need their people "on site"). These managers wanted to see a return back to the way things were.

This has created disruption. Many people have been willing to change jobs and alter their lifestyles to accommodate how THEY want to live their lives. In many cases, frustration with employers and management has increased. Many employees see a lack of fairness.

They believe that they helped and supported management get through the crisis yet see no willingness on management's part to accommodate changes. Many changes that have now been proven to work.

An effective work culture is one where management policies are constantly being reviewed and amended to reflect changes in society. The unwillingness to re-invent or even modify how people undertake their work is a prime example of policies and procedures that block innovation and creativity.

There is no question that a workforce all coming to the workplace every workday is easier to plan and manage. But managing people is not supposed to be easy.

If organizations REALLY believe "people are their greatest asset" or other glib phrases, then they need to recognize the shift in reality. This is making the management and motivation of the workforce more challenging. Requiring better leadership and different approaches to planning and management.

Think of the opportunity of recognizing these changes as blockages in the culture screen and start to clean them out. "Clean the screen." Investigate and eliminate any workplace barriers that start to block the culture screen.

7 Poor management and leadership

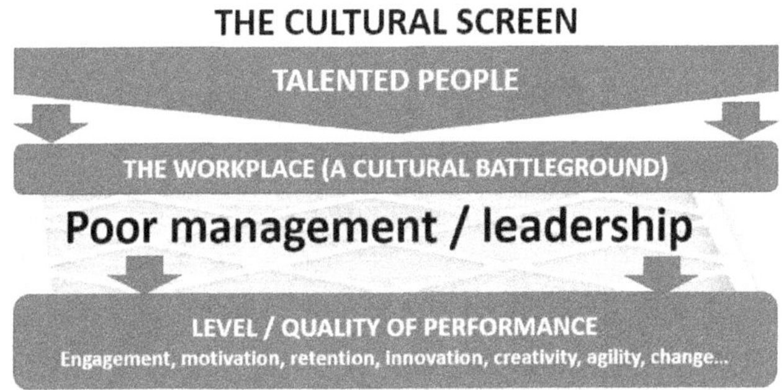

Issue.

Leadership can be considered the glue that holds the network of resources together in the workplace. Leaders manage tasks. If leaders fail to provide a clear understanding of the organization's purpose linked to the employees' own efforts, it will start to block the screen.

Leaders also manage relationships. If leaders fail to behave in a way that is consistent with organizational expectations this is a problem. If leaders fail to collaborate and cooperate and build positive relationships with others this will also block the culture screen.

Problems occur when leaders fail to address the above issues. They also fail when through ineffective communications (including listening) to employees, or failing to provide coaching, support, empathy, consideration and other "expected behaviors." These failures will be compounded if those in leadership positions have a lack of self-awareness. Collectively, these will create a growing lack of engagement and increasing blockages on the culture screen.

Action.

Start with effective leadership selection and development. This includes focusing at least equally on leadership skills as on management skills. Choosing leaders who can balance both their job of task – getting the work done," and relationships that build an effective work culture. Also, don't make management the only career progression path.

Ensure that every leader has a core responsibility of managing and sustaining effective relationships between all people. Adopt selection, review and feedback approaches that incorporate an "understanding of self." Support and encourage openness in giving and receiving feedback related to relationships aspects of the leader's role.

Discussion.

Management effectiveness, and in particular leadership skills are at the heart of organizational culture. While traditional management teaching focused on five key roles including leadership, many management theories today have a longer shopping list.

Let's simplify the whole discussion into two main themes. First a manager is the link between organizational goals and objectives and the work that needs to be done to achieve these. This includes areas like planning, organizing, controlling, and measuring performance. Part of planning is understanding, obtaining, developing, and motivating the people needed to achieve the work.

This second aspect is where leadership comes in. Managers have a choice in how they approach getting the work done:

- **Command and control**. Based on the manager's own knowledge and experience the staff receive instructions about what to do, and how to do it.
- **Inclusivity.** Ensuring everyone understands the task and their role in achieving it, the manager and his team collaborate to get the job done.

Leadership skills impact how the work will be done – the approach to engaging with the people to achieve the task. For many managers inclusivity is harder. It may expose them to admitting "they don't know" about certain technical details. It may also require them to accept that in some cases their team members actually know how to achieve a task better than they do. They will also have to be open to discussion and questioning by the people they work with.

They will have to exercise patience and understanding. They might have to deal with emotional responses. They will have to coach and support rather than direct and control. ***Just telling them what to do might appear easier for the manager.***

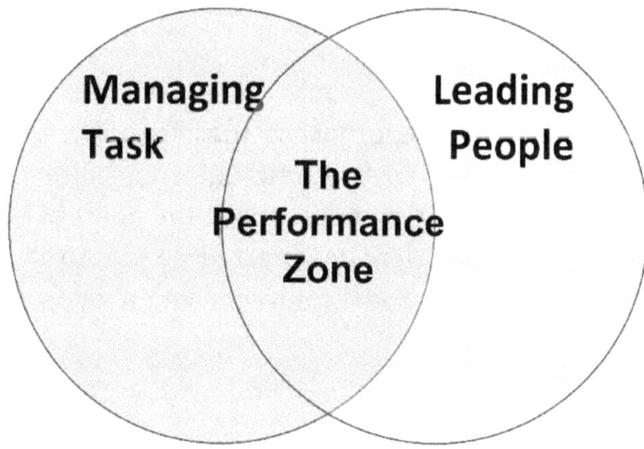

How well an individual in a leadership position "executes" their responsibilities and accountabilities depends on their ability to focus on both “task” and “relationships.” The “performance zone” is where these two responsibilities are optimized. What are some important topics that impact the culture screen?

Failures to communicate.
Communications is cited as one of the most critical yet most difficult aspects of corporate activity.

There are many aspects to effective communications. Often the “economical” approach of improving communications by having “town hall” meetings is cited as “one way to fix our communications problems.” But it is FAR more complex than that.

In the same way that treating people fairly requires time, effective communications require many approaches that cannot be just optimized around the lowest possible cost. Communication affects both task execution and relationship development. It is at the heart of both what we need to do and the behavior that is expected as we do it. One-on-one relationships between people is the “front-line” when it comes to culture.

First – what is communications.

Principally it is the giving and receiving of information. But that involves two people being “on the same wavelength.” Because of the economical approach to saving time – wanting to “get communications done,” potentially both the message being delivered and the receipt of said information can be misinterpreted.

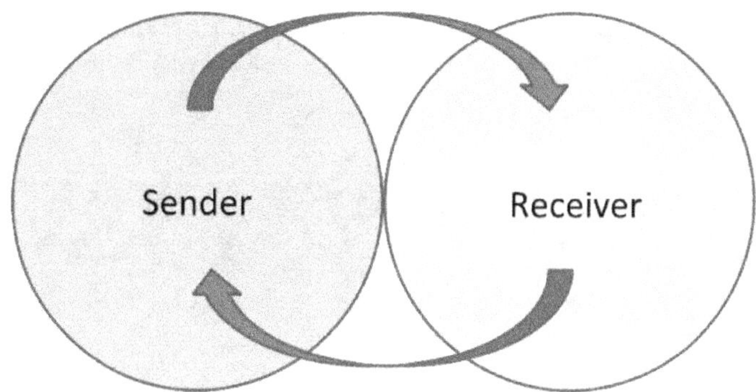

Both sender and receiver have to be fully engaged in the conversation. Being able to communicate effectively while multi-tasking is a myth; something in the exchange will suffer and be "short changed." Skills that both sender and receiver need include:

- **Clarity** of spoken word (a challenge in a multicultural world).
- **Mutual understanding** - ensuring that the message delivered in the message received.
- **Truthful** - telling the truth honestly and clearly.
- **Active listening** - effective listening skills.
- **Clarifying** - asking questions to affirm and clarify understanding.
- **Body language** awareness – do expressions and actions appear to support and reinforce the spoken word?

Poor communication leads to incorrect assumptions and expectations; failure to execute – to turn intent into reality; danger of damaging relationships – and many others.

A culture screen can be kept clean by ensuring clear communications. What is the medium to be used? What is the message to be delivered? What media does the receiver prefer?

The last point is CRITICAL and ties into the need to develop inter-personal understanding. Certain personalities like small talk – others dislike it. If you deliver a message in a style that others dislike, the chances are the message will not be heard. This is why trying to rely on high level, global generic communications to build culture is a mistake.

To be good at communications you have to care about people.

This brings us to the next discussion area on management and leadership. For some this may be a bit contentious but bear with it!

Understanding human behavior

It was once suggested to me that to be a good manager you had to have experience of being the parent of a teenager. Having three children I certainly realized what they meant – although I would not place it as a pre-requisite for those who aspire to management.

Those who provide their impressions and opinions honestly can be brutal but valuable. Teenagers do this. This is where the importance of self-awareness for anyone in a leadership position comes in.

Psychology is critical to the workplace. It helps managers at all levels of organizations select, support, motivate and train employees. It also helps businesses design products, build better workspaces and foster healthy behavior.
American Psychological Association

A person is unaware, when they have no idea how other people "see you", or "hear you" or how you "come across" to them in terms of what you say, how you say, what body language you display, what nuances there may be to how you explain things.

Unless a manager is aware of this, they will not understand why people respond or react the way they do. This goes way beyond team building programs and should permeate every aspect of human development, especially for those in leadership positions. Training and application in self-awareness are critical skills when applied to:

- Recruitment, selection and hiring of staff.
- Selection and development of ANY leader.
- Development of people's groups skills including:
    - Personal learning and development.
    - Team development.
    - Development of partnerships (suppliers / others).
    - Problem solving and conflict resolution.
- Integrating new people into existing work teams.

It is beyond this book to delve further into this science, but in managers are to have the necessary leadership skills, understanding human behaviour has become a "must have" requirement. (See chapter fourteen, Psychology in the workplace).

Absence of trust

The most important role for a manager is to develop, manage and enhance positive relationships. Organizations are complex networks of inter-related people. Every person is or should be trying to collaborate and cooperate to get the job done. Positive relationships are key between:

- Managers and their staff (subordinates)
- Managers and other managers (peers)
- Managers staff and staff elsewhere (cross functional)
    - Internally and externally that form part of the workforce
- All levels in an organizational hierarchy.

This is again not a new development. "The Speed of Trust (This changes everything)" was a 2018 book by Stephen M. R. Covey (son of the also famous Stephen R. Covey who wrote "The 7 Habits of Highly Effective People."

His book explained how trust—and the speed at which it is established with clients, employees, and all stakeholders—is the single most critical component of a successful leader and organization. He stated that:

> *"Trust is "the most overlooked, misunderstood, underutilized asset to enable performance. Its impact, for good or bad, is dramatic and pervasive. It's something you can't escape."*

He continues, *"...Why trust? The simple, often overlooked fact is this: work gets done with and through people. 'The Speed of Trust' offers an unprecedented and eminently practical look at exactly how trust functions in every transaction and every relationship—from the most personal to the broadest, most indirect interaction. It specifically demonstrates how to establish trust intentionally so that you and your organization can forego the time-killing, bureaucratic check-and-balance processes that is so often deployed in lieu of actual trust."*

Effective relationships are based on building trust. Poor cultures are work environments where trust fails to gain traction. Where the actions of people create distrust. Behaviour by leaders is a core part of building trust. But managers are also responsible for calling out and dealing with issues and problems in the workplace that can cause distrust.

Trust is not automatic and is usually driven by personal experience. Those who have had bad experiences from trusting others may grow reluctant to trust as time progresses. They may be personal experiences that are brought into the workplace and will affect workplace behaviour.

One exercise that is used in team development is where a person allows themselves to fall backwards, with the assumption they will be caught by others. Sure, this is great fun – but does it really build trust?

Compare it to a situation where people have a long experience of working together, day in, day out and have found out that over time they can indeed trust their work associates. Small situations. Single events that contribute to a pattern over time. It is the same in personal relationships – it takes time.

Trust is built between people and should not be assumed. Sadly, many people live in societies where trust is not a natural "way things are." Living in repressive, authoritarian regimes can make people suspicious and not trusting.

An unwillingness to trust can develop from living in personal relationships where trust is low. Trust is also limited, when individuals have experienced workplaces where managers and supervisors cannot be trusted – where management hides the truth or fails to communicate and where co-workers are always seeking to shift the blame for problems.

All these personal experiences are brought into the workplace and impact how individuals behave. Creating a safe workplace environment depends on creating a culture where trust can either be reinforced and supported or for some nurtured, developed and assured.

This is the job of leadership – to create that climate. Here are a few questions that may help determine whether trust is a "blocker" in the culture screen.

- Do people believe that management has a "hidden agenda?"
- Is there a gap between what is said and what is actually done?
- Do managers admit when they make a mistake?
- Do managers and others openly ask each other for help?
- Does the manager tend to "coach and support?"
- Do people talk about "we" or is it about "me?"
- Are misunderstandings openly dealt with and discussed?
- Do known behaviour problems get dealt with?

Trust in the workplace is impacted by changes in leadership, changes to staff, strategic shifts in the business and many other activities. Like all the other factors related to creating and sustaining a positive culture that maximize the flow of talent and other resources, trust needs constant reinforcement and is inter-dependent with other factors such as communication.

The Blame Game.

Another outcome of poor management and leadership is "the blame game." This is where people fear that telling the truth will have negative personal repercussions.

Every organization has problems and surprises. Even though processes may be planned and designed, things do go wrong. The major driver of the blame game is fear. Fear if one admits to mistakes. Fear of repercussions.

Fear of being singled out for ridicule. Admittedly irrational, emotional reactions but feelings that are real to the person affected.

It's the same problem as not putting your hand up in school and getting laughed at. People often say never volunteer. But it is serious because for many people the risk may be a fear of not having a job. So, for many, trying to shift blame to someone or something else is better than the risk of expressing an opinion or telling the truth.

There is no limit to those who fear effects. Managers can fear losing a bonus; employees can fear a bad review and being "singled out" when layoffs occur; women and minorities fear because of increased harassment or people assuming they can take advantage of the situation. Fear breeds a desire not to be held responsible or accountable.

Can I tell the truth?
Will my opinion be valued?
Do others want to hear the truth?

Many years ago, when quality management was undergoing a major strategic shift, understanding the root cause of problems was a critical part of being able move forward.

It used to be believed that when problems occurred it was usually that people had made mistakes – the blame was assumed to fall on the employee. But it was soon realized that about 85% of problems that occurred were process related problems and not "people caused" issues.

If you cannot obtain an honest answer or people's opinions on what went wrong and how to fix it, an organization will never be able to operate effectively. Maybe a few questions to think about whether a workplace has an issue with blame and truth telling.

- Are people afraid to raise issues?
- Do managers and supervisors encourage and support feedback?
- Do people who raise problems get branded as "troublemakers?"
- Do people tend to follow rules and avoid decisions to try and stay "out of trouble?"
- Is the "rumor mill" active and believed by people?

These are just a few suggestions that may indicate that the "blame game" might be "alive and well' in an organization.

The perception or reality of unfairness

Another issue that results from poor management and leadership (and which is made worse by areas such as lack of trust, misaligned policies, and procedures and "failure to integrate,") is unfairness. One of the major challenges with unfairness is that in many situations, it is a perception.

People see actions being taken and do not have all the facts, resulting in an incorrect assumption of unfairness. This is why open communications and transparency are so important. Then people can ask for clarification.

The world isn't fair
Get over it.

Some people, including managers believe that the world isn't fair and that people who think it is, need to get over it and accept the fact that you "get what you fight for." This creates a climate of competition not collaboration.

Then again there are many cases of unfairness that really do exist. Several are tied to other aspects of the culture screen. Some decisions are made in compliance with the law, but many are not based on legality but on "socially acceptable behaviour." These decisions may be either morally or ethically based.

The challenge is that fairness is often the result of a judgement decision. These often require some level of guidance to help "do what is right."

Following the law	**Doing what's right**
Legal compliance decisions	**Moral / ethical based decisions**

For many organizations the issue of fairness is a difficult dilemma. There is an assumption that compliance with the law is a requirement (although there remain literally thousands of court cases where organizations fail to comply with employment law).

Many countries and regions have introduced legislation that deals with employment equity. As an example, the requirement for equal pay. The challenge is that in reality some organizations rely on the marketplace only, to determine compensation levels offered to women versus men.

One recent UK court case revealed that a woman who was hired in a senior position, at 70% of the salary that a man working with her was getting for the same position – and she only realized that after she was hired. What happened to employment equity? How did she feel?

Many organizations might argue that if a person agrees to come to work for that amount of money, then why should we give them more? After all the person accepted the position and was willing to work for that amount.

Challenges such as reliance on the marketplace to determine pay levels could lead to feelings of unfairness. Should an organization pay people the lowest level possible – either market based on minimum wage or should starting pay be set at a "living wage" level?

Fairness is not a legal compliance requirement. It is a moral and ethical decision. The challenge is that if the competition only focuses only compliance with the law, does that give them a competitive advantage over those who "do the right thing?" Especially in some jurisdictions, if managers spend shareholder money on something outside of legal compliance, they risk facing being challenged to justify the decision.

This issue of fairness combines with equality / equity but is also discussed later in discrimination and harassment. Treating people fairly is a MAJOR challenge for management – not just from a legal and moral perspective, but because there is a BIG difference between treating people equally (equality) and fairly.

- Treating people equally means that you are doing the same thing for everyone.
- Treating people fairly means that you are doing the right thing for that person, so you are meeting their individual needs.

For management, treating people equally is much easier. "The workforce" can be seen as a generically similar group of (human) resources that are hired as a part of the business model and managed “as a group.” Policies and procedures are put in place – supported by the law – to ensure people are treated equally.

However, while this makes the job of “managing” people easier, it also assumes that people ARE generic and will respond to the same stimulus (like robots). This is increasingly being recognized as unrealistic. Not only do people make judgements about fairness based on emotional responses, but they also interpret fairness individually in different ways.

This is one reason why corporate values, as an underpinning of a code of ethics, have become so important. Shared values among the workforce will tend to create a better foundation for understanding expectations of fairness.

This means that an organization that seeks to effectively manage its’ workforce will have to strike the balance between equity and flexibility. Certainly, there must be rules, policies, and procedures but there must be some allowance for situational flexibility – because situations people are placed in are often not equal.

Here are some thoughts about how fairness needs to be strategically addressed in an organization:

- Remember that “fair” doesn't mean equal or “the same.”
- Always be kind to people and see them as an individual.
- Practice active listening with people to understand their perspective.
- Seek out and understand contextual / situational differences.
- Demonstrate empathy and compassion – but
- Seek out an understanding of how the person wants to be treated.
- Remember that understanding doesn't mean agreeing.
- Seek resolutions based on “intent” of the policy but “fairness of interpretation.”

- Beware of creating precedents that cannot be sustained / copied.

This approach means that "people related" policies and procedures must be developed with an expectation of the need for some level of interpretation. While HR may devise these, managers and supervisors have to implement them.

For this to work, these managers must have adequate delegated authority to make situational decisions. (This is why successful organizations that have created solid "people-centric workplaces", focus attention on the supervisor / employee relationship – such as Toyota.)

Addressing the need for effective leadership

Unless the desire for a positive work culture is planned and driven from the board level and is considered strategically critical, problems will remain, because with no guidance, managers will make different decisions.

Often owners, the board and often senior leadership believe that they already are managing towards a positive culture. There are plaques on the wall extolling the virtues and values of the organization. Lofty statements are made by the CEO at town hall meetings. Annual reports and shareholder meetings assure owners that management is ensuring a positive workplace culture.

But this is not the world that most of the workforce lives in. This is not their reality. The larger the organization the more risk of this problem exists. What often gets in the way?

- No high-level strategic guidance on values / behavior
- Wrong managers in place – nonbelievers
- Poor hiring and promotion approaches, that do not address leadership behaviors.
- Career development frameworks, where promotion can only be achieved by "going into management." (Some great technical

experts are promoted to managers because it's the only way that they can earn more – but they either don't like it or are bad at leadership skills).

- Inadequate development of managers (budgets too tight, funds not available).
- Inconsistent development of managers – no clear statement of expectations, different organizations used to support development who use different terminology, models, and approaches.
- Manager development seen as an "event" not a continual process.
- No structured coaching of managers and leaders.
- Performance feedback does not address behaviors that can create a negative culture ("screen issues").
- Managerial performance issues not being addressed.

Managers are "the glue that holds the culture together." They are the ones that convert intent into reality.

A final Word.

Two suggestions based on my experience as a President trying to make change happen.

1. The Middle Manager Dilemma.

Yes - you, as the leader, may be right, and change is needed. You may be right that most employees want to see the changes that you want to make put in place. BUT you find that your greatest problem is convincing "middle managers."

DO NOT in any situation try and go around your middle managers to make the desired changes happen. These managers are the ones that manage the day-to-day work of the employees and also do their performance reviews and promotions. They are ultimately the ones that will make it work or not. Your middle managers (and all others) MUST be fully on board the culture train. It must "cascade" from the top down.

2. But it's taking so long.

Correct. An example comes from when I asked one of my managers, (who was one of my "change champions"), why things were taking so long. "People want to see these changes - I know that" I said. "So why isn't this happening?" "Well," he replied. "Until you became President, everybody kept their head down and followed instructions. Now you want them to put their hand up and openly volunteer. You have to realize that this is like peace after the war. They have been keeping their head down in the trenches. You came along, wave the white flag, and say it's OK so put your head out now. One will look at the other and say – you go first. I will wait and see if your head gets shot off. Maybe if nothing happens to you, I may start to believe."

People will believe what you demonstrate NOT what you say (until they really trust you). Telling them things have changed or will change is NEVER enough. They will always say "show me."

8 Failure to integrate.

Issue

Organizations are created to achieve a purpose. The core task of management is to create a system capable of integrating all the required resources, that operates at an optimum level. Functional responsibility and silos often get in the way of this happening. Relationships should be mutually supportive and collaborative with everyone working towards a common goal. So often personal, departmental, and functional priorities are allowed to get in the way of this happening.

Blockages occur when people fail to work together towards a common goal. Sometimes this is structural (poor organization and planning) and sometimes it is operational (poor execution). Both create blockages in the culture screen and cause frustration and disengagement.

Action

Start at the senior level by building a collaborative approach to the achievement of organizational goals and less focus on individual "silo based" achievements. Instill flexibility into resource management to encourage shifting and sharing of resources. Encourage collaboration efforts "down, through and across" the organization.

Encourage approaches that offer opportunities to build cross functional relationships (internally and externally). Provide career development opportunities across silos.

Discussion

Once again this is not a new issue – although from all the talk about integrated thinking and integrated reporting, one would be led to believe that it was the latest and greatest management idea.

An organization is a system

An organization is established for a purpose. In order to achieve that purpose, management's task is to bring together all the necessary resources and integrate them into a system that can produce the desired outputs and outcomes. The unique business model that every organization creates.

The workplace is where this all happens. Where people become connected with each other and all the other people who are involved in "the business processes." The "system" that converts inputs to outputs and creates the desired outcomes (results).

Financial control is traditionally silo based with planning and control exercised by each function. What is required is a system-based approach.

Think of it like an orchestra, or a pit crew at a motor race, or a sports team.

A successful organization is one where the required resources are obtained and then brought together in the optimum way to create the desired results. The more effectively the system operates the more valuable it can become. One factor that impacts the ability of the system to work at an optimum level is decision making based purely on financial criteria. As an example, the lowest cost supplier may not make the best working partner in the relationship aspects. (Can we work with these people?)

Each of the parts or resources that have been brought together must be working at their highest level of possible performance, seamlessly creating the desired outputs.

A great organization is one where the managers do this so well that they create a competitive advantage. In order to achieve this on a sustainable basis, the organization must develop and sustain a great workplace culture.

The workplace can be called "the crucible" within which all the "ingredients" of the business model come together to react, in order to create the desired outputs and outcomes. Leaders hold the crucible in their hands.

With all the recent talk about integration, a helpful framework was developed[5], that clarifies the resources used in an integrated business system. Managements' task is to acquire and integrate a combination of these resources to optimize the outcome of their business system or model. The core resources in this framework (somewhat simplified) are:

- Financial capital. Money is needed.
- Manufactured capital. Organizations need to buy equipment.
- Human capital. The workforce – people who do stuff.
- Intellectual capital. Knowledge.
- Relationship / social capital. Other inter-dependencies.
- Natural capital. The availability of "free" resources.

These are like the ingredients of a world class food dish that a chef may prepare. They seek their ingredients that are "fit for purpose" but that are also available at a competitive price that will allow them to serve their dish at a price people can afford. Preparing the dish is then a process of integration – using all of the resources available – equipment, people, the skills, and knowledge of people and so on.

IN addition to these categories of "capitals" being shown as resource inputs, each one also has outputs and outcomes. These can be helpful in understanding the "total system outcomes" that impact more than financial capital.

As an example, what impact is there on the environment as a result of the integration taking place? Pollution? Waste? For people – what's the impact? They get paid but are there zero accidents? Are they healthy – mentally and physically?

---

[5] Originally the International Integrated Reporting Committee IIRC, 2013 et. seq.

Starting with Purpose.
As discussed in the last chapter, managers are the people who manage and control integration. What do they, and the people who work for them, need to know what their purpose, goals and objectives are, so that they can do a good job.

CLARITY OF PURPOSE

Two of the most important questions come from ensuring that every single resource – especially every single person, knows about an organizations Purpose.

1. WHAT are we trying to do here, and
2. How do I fit into achieving this. (What is expected of me).

This concept of integration centers around purpose. An effective organization is one that is "fit for purpose."

There is a centrality to the theme of both a stated and clear purpose, and a shared and understood purpose. Every resource required in the business model is required based on the organizations' purpose.

Many will know that the late Frederick Winslow Taylor became famous in the days of industrial engineering and mass production. A time when every task was broken down to its lowest component and everyone's work was individually designed. The purpose was translated down to the machines and equipment and the steps that people performed at each stage to get the work done. The process of task integration was defined and managed.

At that time America led the world in commercial industrialization. Even the Japanese visited the USA to learn how to build effective manufacturing processes.

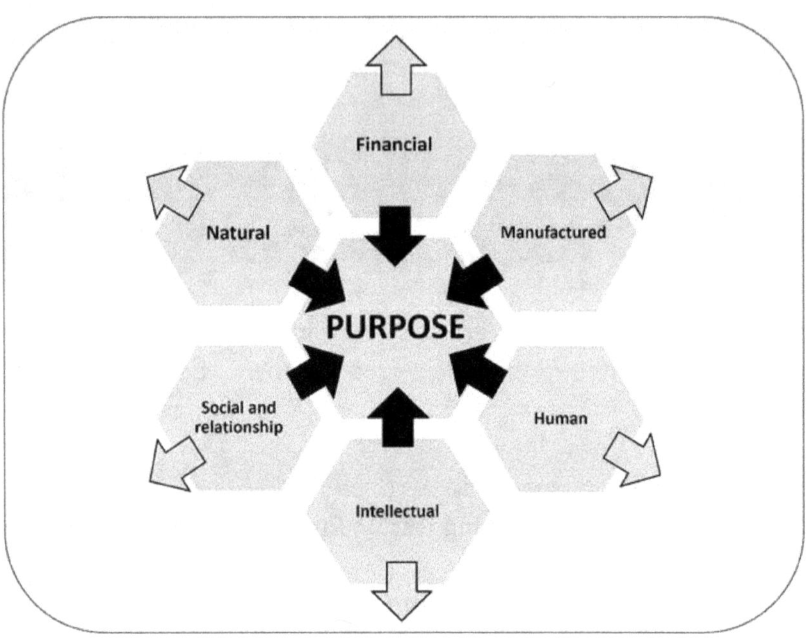

But over time, it was learned that understanding, designing, developing, and managing the processes through which the required purpose was to be achieved, could only be done by taking a systems approach. This was at the heart of understanding "the system" and the concept of integration. ALL the parts have to be operating together.

It also led to understanding of the theory of constraints. Basically, the system can only produce at the level defined by the resource with the greatest limited capacity.

The quality revolution of the 1980's started a renewed focus on integrated systems thinking. This was further developed when the concept of integrated thinking was developed as the foundation of integrated reporting. The latter came about because of the emerging growth of corporate reports providing information on non-financial aspects of performance.

Managers had already moved towards an integrated thinking approach, strongly reinforced by the development of performance dashboards or "balanced scorecards[6]." Performance measurement systems were already moving beyond financial metrics to the reporting of factors determining the health of the "underlying system."

> **"Integrated thinking can help create a virtuous loop of integration within an organization across functional siloes. Businesses that are in this integrated thinking loop are on a continuous journey, evaluated through a management and reporting philosophy that results in ongoing performance improvements."**
>
> ***IFAC Knowledge Gateway***

This evolution of integrated thinking, started with corporate social responsibility (CSR), through to include "people, planet, and profit," and then integrated reporting or <IR> based on the IIRC framework discussed earlier.

In promoting their approach to integration, the IIRC developed a model of organizational operations. At the center of the schematic shown in Figure 1, is the business model that integrates all of the inputs on the left and creates outputs and outcomes on the right. This is "the system."

---

[6] The Balanced Scorecard, Kaplan & Norton, Harvard Business Press

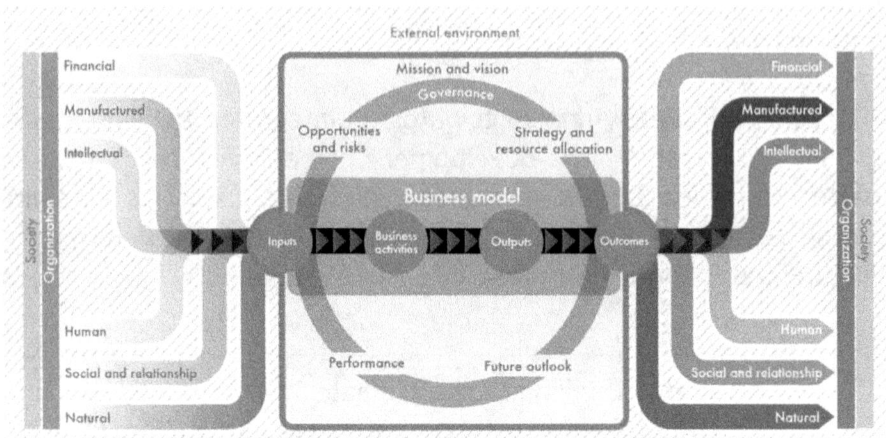

Figure 1 IIRC Process through which value is created, preserved, or eroded.

The quote above from IFAC (The International Federation of Accountants), identifies "integration across functional silos." This aspect of integration – or lack of it, is the core of problems with the culture screen and integrated thinking.

Unless all functions and departments at all levels in the organization are communicating, cooperating, and collaborating "as one system," people working within the system will not be working at their optimum performance level. Plus, they will be personally frustrated.

Business culture and a healthy workplace are the foundations of any business model. Unless the work environment that people are placed in during the process of integration, supports and accelerates their talent, then the performance of the system will be constrained.

The major constraint to performance in the 21st century is a blocked culture screen getting in the way of people's and the systems potential.

9 Irresponsible antisocial behavior

THE CULTURAL SCREEN

TALENTED PEOPLE

THE WORKPLACE (A CULTURAL BATTLEGROUND)

Irresponsible / anti-social behavior

LEVEL / QUALITY OF PERFORMANCE

Engagement, motivation, retention, innovation, creativity, agility, change...

Issue

Organizations are expected to abide by the law. They are also expected to behave responsibly and reflect the values of the society that the organization operates within. Individual and group behaviour often makes this a challenge. This is caused by clashes of personalities, personal beliefs, and values, as well as fear, inconsistent and overlapping goals and other issues.

To create an effective workplace environment, people need to have a level of common and shared expectations of behavior. The place needs to be "safe," both for the individuals well-being and for the optimum collaboration. Without a foundation of acceptable behavior, poor relationships will create significant blockages and disengagement.

Action

Ensure legal compliance moves beyond committing to compliance with the law to firmly embedding expectations of diversity, equity, and inclusion into every facet of operational behavior.

Engage with the workforce to determine expectations of responsible behavior, both legal compliance and generally accepted societal expectations. Embed these within a foundational document such as a values statement, code of ethics or code of conduct. Use this as a basis for recruitment, selection, and orientation of all the workforce. In particular embed this is leadership selection, development, and performance feedback.

Ensure there is a "safe" environment where problems related to behavioral issues can be identified, escalated and resolved.

Discussion

An organization can be considered "a collection of people brought together to achieve a shared purpose."

Within an organization, the way individuals behave is absolutely critical. Plus, the way people behave towards each other, individually or as groups, such as work associates, has a significant impact on well-being, engagement, motivation and performance. On everyone's ability to enjoy work and to function at a high level of performance. Think about behaviour related to the following workplace relationships:

The way "the organization" treats all the employees.

This is usually reflected in its policies and procedures. These policies and procedures reflect the attitudes and behaviors of those in a governance role who decide how the organization will operate based on what their values are. (This is why culture is strategic).

Are people a "resource" or commodity, or are they human beings that are entering into a mutually beneficial relationship with the organization? Do the policies show respect, value and inclusion?

The way that managers within the organization treat those that they have authority over.

Managers will typically follow policies and procedures. However, they often have some degree of discretion in how these are applied. These are the relationships where either a "command and control" approach is applied or a collaborative, inclusive and supportive approach.

While some aspects of this relationship will be determined by pre-defined approaches such as compliance with policies and procedures, the personality, values, biases, and emotional "state" of the individual manager will also have a significant impact.

Leadership development programs, especially in the area of inter-personal skills, will provide some level of guidance on the expected behavior of managers towards those that the supervise. Examples would include harassment, bullying, communications, and others.

The way that individuals who work together treat each other – such as work teams and peer groups.

This is often a principle focus of team development or team building initiatives. The goal is to enhance the way that people who have to work closely together "get on" with one another.

These relationships can be complicated. While people bring their own personality, bias, emotional state, and values and belief system with them into the workplace, they are also impacted by the behavior of those around them. While people cannot change their personalities, they can adopt modified behaviors based on how the group operates.

The way that people who work within the same organization treat each other (such as inter-departmental).
This is similar to the above but in many cases, there will be a lower level of engagement as the relationships will be intermittent and often between different functional groups.

The approach that seeks to "break down silos" includes addressing the goal of territorial behaviour and eliminating any impact of defensiveness between departments. Building the concept that "we are all on one team here."

One of the challenges in relationships between departments is the tendency for each one to create its' own "fiefdom," often seeing others outside their functional area as "different people." Hence the development of terms like bean counters for the accountants, as a result of applying stereotypes to people who have certain skills sets. This can lead to name calling and demeaning language that is in effect harassment.

The way that people in the organization treat those externally who they work with or are in contact with.
While certain areas or functions may have a dominant role in working with third parties, the networking or relationships is making it increasingly important that internal and external relationships are considered. Are suppliers treated as partners will support and openness? Are customers treated in the same way?

One area of increasing importance is relationships with organizations that provide external services such as IT and accounting. These functions operate as though they are internal, yet they are part of a third-party organization that may have different policies and procedures. They might also have a very different set of values and behavioral expectations. Differences in behavior might create challenges in these areas and lead to blockages in the culture screen.

What behaviors can create a problem?
Wherever poor behavior occurs, it can cause significant "blockages" in the culture screen. What types of issues occur that create these blockages?

Assuming that an organization wishes to function as a responsible member of society, then the way that people behave internally should reflect that same expectation. What are some examples that might be considered irresponsible or anti-social?

Harassment – sexual, physical
Hostility or aggressiveness.
Abusive, offensive, belittling, or threatening behaviour.
Rudeness, disrespect or bullying toward colleagues or clients.
Microaggression.
Argumentative
Lack of empathy or concern for others
Inappropriate physical behaviour (touching, facial expressions).
Avoiding personal accountability or responsibility.
Blaming others
Taking credit for the ideas and work of others
Throwing people "under the bus" to shift blame.
Cutting off or interrupting others
Narcissism
Gossiping about the company or other people
Monopolizing conversations, meetings, and discussions
Passive / aggressive behaviour
Destructive feedback or criticism
Lack of respect or inclusion

Examples of negative behaviour at the collective level can include actions or statements that undermine team motivation or business goals and resistance to change or criticism, especially when it's someone else's idea. Also lying to others or providing knowingly incorrect information.

Behaviour also includes personal conduct related to the "attitude" that some people take towards the workplace. These can include:

Work habits - arriving late and leaving early.
Taking personal calls or being on your phone.
Being dismissive of others (including because of race, color, creed etc.)
Unreasonableness - displaying an unnecessary sense of urgency.
Misuse of company time.
Covering up for someone who is absent or shows up late (altering timesheets).
Making promises then missing deadlines
Failing to communicate issues and problems.

Naturally illegal behaviour would be considered a problem – especially if it is condoned by those in authority. This might include employee theft both of time, materials, or personal use of property.

One quote that stands out comes from Dr. Greg Alston writing in a blog in Multi Briefs. I personally refer to this as "corporate terrorism."

> *"Subversive behavior: subversive behavior is unethical. If you work for a company that you don't agree with, you only have two ethical choices. If you are going to accept the paycheck, then swallow your pride and do the job in the manner requested. If you disagree with the way things are being done, then resign and seek other employment. But you do not have the right to take the paycheck and then undermine the programs of your employer. Subversive behavior is the highest form of evil.*

Some organizations do very little to define expected behaviors, instead leaving it to people to act "how they know to behave." This approach ignores any risk related to unexpected or anti-social behaviour in the workplace. This is the source of significant barriers in the cultural screen.

Organizations seek to establish a foundation of behavior through creating either a code of ethics or a code of conduct. But unless these documents are mutually agreed and practiced, they will mean very little (other than having a plaque on the wall).

In fact, making these statement without ensuring they are embedded into every aspect of relationships and behavior is often worse than doing nothing. Once an organization sets expectations people expect it to turn into reality. When it fails to, levels of de-motivation become more significant.

Some areas of behaviour are now built into mandatory legal requirements in different jurisdictions. However, while an organization may seek to abide by the law in providing training and awareness programs and meeting hiring requirements, REAL application requires that the legal commitment is translated into how people interact with one another every day in every situation.

CIVILITY IN THE WORKPLACE

Ensuring responsible behaviour requires that the workplace reflects what would happen in a "civilized society." People who behave in what is considered an ethical and socially responsible manner.

Business ethics is an evolving topic, especially as it relates to providing guidance for behaviors and relationships. Generally, the following ethical principles are expected: honesty, fairness, (inclusive) leadership, integrity, compassion, respect, responsibility, loyalty, law-abiding, transparency, and responding to environmental concerns.

A number of organizations that provide staff recruitment services, suggest the following five are the most sought-after workplace behaviors:

- Integrity.
- Honesty.
- Discipline.
- Fairness and respect.
- Being responsible and accountable.

But these have to become the way the whole organization operates. As described in a later chapter, this is why governance is so critical in setting the desired expectations of behaviour. Also, why leadership is so critical in re-enforcing the stated expectations.

An effective culture underpins responsible behavior. If decision making is responsible, and behavior is responsible then there is likely a sound foundation for the culture. Irresponsible behavior will cause significant blockages in the culture screen – not just with internal talent but with all people who interact with the business.

Part 2

Aspects, implications, and actions

How the culture screen impacts
other initiatives and strategic goals.

Starting to think about where to focus.

10 Employee engagement

Employee engagement is a measure of how well the organization is creating and sustaining a workplace that supports employees. An understanding of the culture screen and blockages will enhance the understanding of the "levers" management uses to set optimum engagement conditions.

It seems that high on every executive's agenda is trying to enhance employee engagement. Survey after survey demonstrates a correlation between positive levels of employee engagement and organizational performance.

According to Gallup[7] global employee engagement runs at about 22% while in the US it is higher at about 32%. Look at the reverse. About 78% of the global workforce is disengaged at some level. In the US it is 68%. That's terrible. What a waste of human talent.

These annual reports have been produced for almost twenty years and the numbers remain low. In spite of all the attention. An article[8] commenting on the 2022 Gallup report indicated that this waste costs $7.8 trillion annually equivalent to 11% of global GDP.

---

[7] Gallup Q12 Meta-analysis produced annually.

[8] The World's $7.8 Trillion Workplace Problem, Ryan Pendell, June 14th, 2022, Workplace Gallup,

CULTURE DRIVES ENGAGEMENT

ORGANIZATION CULTURE
IS
WHAT EMPLOYEES EXPERIENCE IN THE WORKPLACE WHICH CREATES LEVELS OF EMPLOYEE ENGAGEMENT

It's not actually "rocket science" as they say. Any organization wishing to enhance its level of employee engagement must understand the factors that positively and negatively impact people's feelings about their workplace experience. (In technical terms these are the conditions or antecedents of engagement!)

The culture screen acts as a filter through which the potential of a talented workforce has to pass in order to get their work done and create results.

The cleaner the filter – the less blockages that get in the way, the greater the opportunity for people to work at their maximum potential. The goal of organizational design should be to build a system within which human talent can thrive. From a system perspective the workplace must be "fit for purpose." Clearly, based on the survey data, few workplaces meet this expectation.

Part of the challenge is that few organizations understand, accept or even tolerate the reality that people – human beings, are BOTH rational and emotional.

When an employee answers questions related to their workplace, they are answering with a combination of rational and emotional responses. They are responding based on the "conditions" that they find themselves experiencing.

The traditional model of employee engagement was developed from studies that focused on individual engagement. One of the earliest tools was called the Utrecht Work Engagement Scale (UWES) that was able to ask specific questions related to employee well-being and statistically correlating individual levels of engagement with health symptoms like burnout.

There remains discussion over whether high engagement can also cause burnout. Possibly this would be related to the dangers of ones' addiction to work that could be created if one was "over-engaged." This is the subject of a whole other discussion on "work-life" balance.

With today's increasing focus on employee engagement linked to escalating mental health concerns, creating a positive workplace that results in sustaining healthy individuals is potentially becoming more critical.

Historically a healthy workplace that addresses workplace safety, and many physical requirements are now enshrined in law in many countries. In some more advanced legislation this has now been expanded to include areas like harassment and mental safety and well-being. This traditional approach can be expanded and aligned with the culture screen thinking.

One mantra that organizations have adopted, the embraces many aspects of positive behaviour is "do no harm." This could potentially address several aspects of engagement, as it impacts individuals both physically and mentally. In particular it embraces the behavioral aspects that can create "psychological harm." It's about creating a "safe space" at work.

Much of the traditional work on employee engagement has been captured in an ISO document titled ISO 23326:2022 Human resource management — Employee engagement — Guidelines. This document references a model that shows the following continuum.

Framework for employee engagement		
Conditions / antecedents	Engagement	Potential outcomes (Performance)

Potential outcomes (performance) of an organization are related to the level of employee engagement. (This is why people want to measure engagement. It also complements the reports and studies of organizations such as Gallup).

The definition of employee engagement is in debate although many conceptually understand the concept. *"Employee engagement is the emotional commitment the employee has to the organization and its goals."* (A 2012 definition from Forbes[9]).

An "engaged employee" is defined as one who is fully absorbed by and enthusiastic about their work and so takes positive action to further the organization's reputation and interests. An engaged employee has a positive attitude towards the organization and its values. (2017 source used by Wikipedia[10]).

Conditions or antecedents – a term used in the original model which can also be called drivers (of engagement) are those things that impact an individual's level of engagement.

In terms of organizational culture and the culture screen one can state that "the job of management is to create a work environment where the conditions, antecedents, and drivers are managed in such a way as to optimize the contribution of the individual." The model might appear to

[9] Kevin Kruse, Jun 22, 2012, "What is employee engagement?" Forbes magazine

[10] "Employee Engagement". Emptrust. 5 August 2017. Retrieved 11 August 2017.

show the following – where the "conditions in the workplace" are those shown as potential barriers to engagement – which create a negative culture.

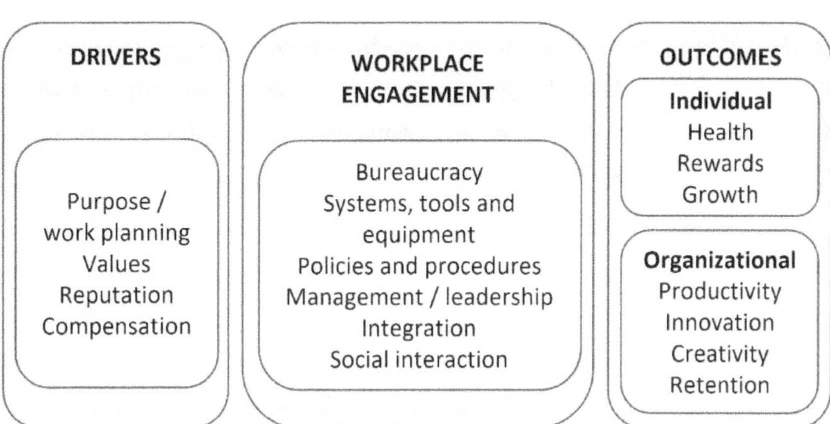

Outcomes are BOTH organizational AND individual. Management has traditionally been more focused on organizational outcomes – principally financial returns and customer acceptance / satisfaction. The impacts that the workplace has on other outcomes – such as individual health, personal growth and a fair wage have been secondary. Government legislation has been enacted in many countries to establish minimum wages.

If an organization fails to consider both types of outcome, its' risk is being unable to attract and retain talented people. The Gallup work to correlate organizational outcomes confirms this and adds to the reality of lower organizational performance related to lower levels of engagement.

Drivers (conditions and antecedents) of engagement might be thought of as the issues that management creates through building its business model. In many cases that is the case. Management designs many of the structures, policies, systems, approaches, and decision making that create and impact the workplace. They define the purpose and determine the organizational structure and work assignments. They buy the tools and equipment. They (should) set the organizational values that determine expected behavior in the workplace.

By their behavior as an organization in the marketplace, they create a positive reputation that can act as an attractor of talent and also a sense of pride. A poor reputation will do the opposite. They also determine policies related to compensation, benefits and other "contractual conditions" with their employees. Many of these are key factors or drivers in determining the level of employee engagement.

Yet there is a greater issue that is often ignored. Employee engagement can also be impacted by personal factors that the organization does NOT directly control.

Consider two examples. First, management cannot "control" behavior in the workplace because people will act as individuals. They will bring with them all their beliefs, biases, experiences, attitudes, and everything else. They will reflect the reality of their own, unique personality. Therefore, when a company hires people, it must get "the right people on the bus."

Secondly, management, in particular in its application of leadership skills, MUST ensure that once people are "on the bus," the actual behavior that takes place in the workplace is considered acceptable. If people are allowed "to get away with" poor behavior, employee engagement will be negatively impacted.

People "bring their whole self to work." This will result in personal issues that are impacting an individual's life "spilling over" into their emotional behavior in the workplace. This is why programs such as EAP (Employee Assistance Programs) or EAR (Employee Assistance Resources) are so important.

Employee engagement is a complex mixture of rational and emotional responses, based on both personal belief's values and feelings, underpinned by conditions that management creates PLUS the reality of each individual's own personal life experience. WOW. No wonder employee engagement is such a complex issue.

Employee engagement has been quoted as being "...a human resources (HR) concept that describes the level of enthusiasm and dedication a worker feels toward their job[11]." IT is NOT just an HR concept.

Famously, Peter Drucker once said that "culture eats strategy for breakfast." Because employee engagement is critical to organization performance and the well-being of the workforce (and others who are a part of the business model), this quote can possibly now be modified.

Culture doesn't just eat strategy for breakfast.

CULTURE IS STRATEGY

Culture is about creating a work environment where people thrive. This is a central part of strategy. Unless culture is planned and managed it will evolve without planning, control, measurement, and management.

Culture will be "the way we do things around here" not because it is planned and managed but because it has developed based on the evolution of what is supported and allowed.

The six aspects of blockages in the workplace presented in the culture screen are foundations for understanding employee engagement. Measurement of employee engagement is important, but what is CRITICAL is the ability to understand the linkages between conditions that management creates for employees and their level of engagement.

---

[11] Investopedia extracted April 6th, 2023.

For culture to be strategically planned and managed, the necessary conditions must be planned and implemented so that they form the drivers.

High employee engagement is a measure of a positive workplace. Talented people can be hired, well-paid and their skills utilized but unless the workplace "leverages" those capabilities, the individual and collective outcomes will be sub-optimized.

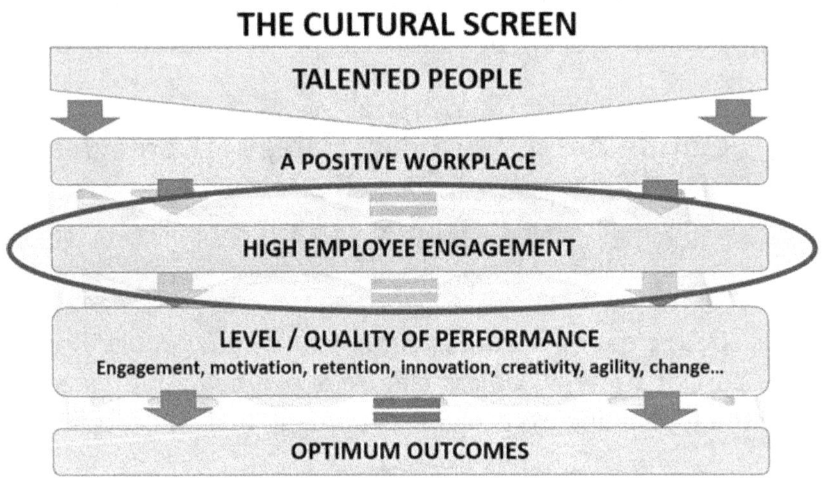

11 The critical role of leadership

Leadership is in the construction business. Leaders are either builders of people or are in the demolition business.

Think of leaders – that is people in leadership positions as having a "sacred trust." First related to their investors. For many leaders, they are acting on behalf of other people who are the owners. Those who are the investors in the organization.

As a leader, an individual holds personal responsibility for both protecting their investors' money and in generating a return on their investment. Leaders are being trusted by the investors to "do the right thing."

Many organizations already recognize this and place investors or shareholders as their main priority. The challenge is that to protect the shareholders' interests,' leaders must also protect all aspects related to how their shareholders' money is spent.

Leaders can no longer look at the financial records to determine "where the investors' money went." It used to be that the investors' money showed up on the balance sheet in terms of either the cash that was invested, or the assets that had been purchased or created through the day-to-day activity of the business.

Not anymore. Today's financial records only reflect about 5% of the "value" of an organization. That's because all the shareholder money that has been spent on hiring, developing, and training the work force has been treated as an expense and written off. It's not seen as an asset."

Likewise, money spent on developing the supply chain and the suppliers has been written off. The costs incurred to build those critical supply relationships have become critical to an organization's sustainability.

Same with customer relationships. All that time and effort to identify, develop and sustain the customer base has been written off as an expense. All the advertising and marketing costs that "build the brand." All written off.

The point is that the "sacred trust" that a leader has, is to protect not just the visible assets but the invisible ones – those that are referred to as intangibles. Those things that an investor, if they had to purchase the organization, would have to pay for. The cost being the market value of the business.

This market value represents the value of the system that management has created, that leaders need to protect, guide, sustain and nurture. The value of the system that has been created that creates a return for investors BUT is also being managed and protected for sustainability into the future (maintaining its' ability to be a "going concern.")

Not only do leaders have a sacred trust to look after the TOTAL value of the shareholders organization – they hold the well-being of many people and organizations in their hands.

The decisions that leaders make will not only affect the financial "wealth" of the investor but will have a critical impact on the well-being and lives of everyone of their employees and their families. The health of the communities within which they operate. The businesses of their customers and suppliers, as well as their continued well-being and health.

While protecting the environment and climate change may seem new for many, in reality it has always been part of the sacred trust of leaders. To make sure that not only are their investors interests protected, but that they no "no harm" to those that they impact including the planet within which we all live and depend upon.

DO NO HARM

The mantra of a leader who understands the depth of their sacred trust and their position of responsibility

All aspects of "do no harm" are critical, but the greatest intersection of this between the stakeholders involved and the investors who provide the money, is the people. People not only provide physical labor they provide mental capability; this mental capability includes intellectual capital that is central to innovation and creativity.

The intersection occurs because typically the single largest annual expenditure that an organization makes is to pay people. This is on top of the money they spend to attract, develop, and retain them. (The greater the employee turnover, the greater the hidden losses).

PEOPLE ARE OUR GREATEST ASSETS
Except they are not financial assets and the business does not own them.

People are a major risk for any organization and that risk is largely managed by those in a leadership position. The effectiveness of the workplace that leaders create and sustain is central to human effectiveness including risk mitigation. It is also a core driver of employee engagement and culture.

A poor or less healthy culture has two different impacts – both of which are extremely negative.

The disengaged workforce
We have already seen by some estimates, that dis-engaged employees' number between 68% of the workforce in the US and 78% globally. These are the people in the business that remain in place, and whose engagement, motivation, productivity and performance are sub-optimal.

While they are still being paid, the company "labor ROI" is lower. This organizational impact is increasingly being measured by a calculation called HC-ROI (Human Capital Return on Investment). While there are pros and cons to this measurement, at the gross level it does indicate where there are opportunities for improvement.

As discussed earlier, many of the issues identified as being part of the culture screen are the drivers of both engagement and disengagement. Determining what these are and fixing the problem, is the job of leadership.

If it is not fixed it will have negative impacts on outcomes. As an example, a negative outcome for investors, in terms of BOTH their annual earnings as well as their risk of sustaining the value of their investment. For individuals a negative outcome in terms of de-motivation and possible poor health issues, as well as lack of opportunity and growth. These will lead to poor productivity and loss of innovation and creativity.

The loss of workforce
Because people are not "owned" by the organization, they can decide to just "walk out of the door." Can they be replaced? Yes – but there will be an impact both on loss of accumulated investment, a drop in productivity, a repeated learning curve, a need to re-build relationships – and more.

In the past when employees provided "just" physical labor which was often unskilled, they were more easily replaced. That is no longer true. People are still replaceable but the impact on the organization is significant – both financially and operationally.

Financially this problem will result in higher rates of employee turnover or loss. Additionally, the losses will likely be the more talented people who are attractive to other employers.

Failure to attract talent.
A workplace where there is a disengaged workforce will probably be less successful in attracting new talent. People will not recommend friends and reviews on sites such as Glassdoor will be less positive.

Some organizations assess their ability "to be attractive" by measuring NPI or Net Promoter Score. Originally aimed at assessing client satisfaction this can also be an indicator of whether employees would promote the company to friends as a great place to work, and to people in the community as to whether the organization was a great company or somewhat less so.

Criticality of leadership
Clearly those in leadership positions are both creators of an organizations "way of doing things" as well as an enabler of optimizing the productive application of all resources. So much of this is about enabling talent internally and relationships both internally and externally.

Leadership "makes it happen." But what about the challenge the people in leadership positions have in spending the necessary time on people "issues." What about the balance between getting the job done and taking the time to coach and support staff?

Even more challenging is the question about the support that comes from "the top" in terms of achieving the balance needed? Individual leaders may be fully committed to creating a great culture, but if the total "system" does not make this a strategic priority, can an effective culture ever be sustained?

Are leaders headed in the wrong direction?

Is it clearly evident that leaders recognize this important shift? Is more time and effort being placed on the selection, training and development of leaders? Most importantly, is the need for managers to increase their time commitment in their leadership role taking place? The answer is no. The focus on tasks is reducing the focus on people and relationships.

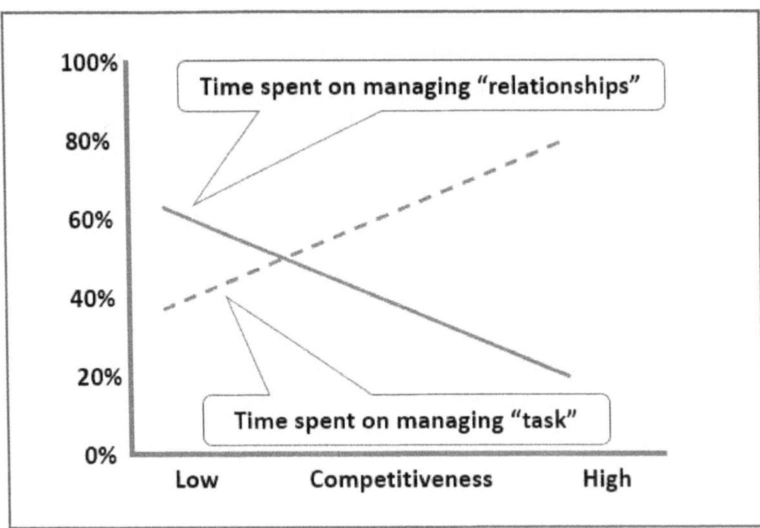

Many managers – especially those in mid-management positions are becoming the "meat in the sandwich." Increasing competitiveness in the marketplace requires that organizations constantly seek ways to cut costs. Many have removed layers of middle-managers in the drive for greater agility and flexibility.

What has often happened is that managers have been required to take on more "actual task work." The time for this can only come from two places. Either working longer hours – impacting work / life balance and potentially social and health problems. Or managers find themselves spending less time on leadership aspects of building and nurturing relationships – impacting the quality and effectiveness of the relationships.

At a time when leadership aspects of a manager's responsibility are increasing in importance, the reality is that for many their actual time spent on these aspects is decreasing.

This quote from the Future Forum 2022 report titled "Executives feel the strain of leading in the "new normal" seems to suggest that managers are feeling the pain. *"Of all office workers, middle managers are reporting the highest levels of stress and anxiety and the worst work-life balance. Slack Technologies Inc.'s Future Forum, found a record 43% of managers say they're burned out — the highest of any job level."* This report looks at all managers, and at all levels the problem is increasing.

Headline[12].
"Middle managers are so burned out that nearly half want to quit within the next year."

These problems translate into personal health issues. The Workforce Institute at UKG report "Mental Health at Work: Managers and Money" published in 2023 stated the following. *"One in five employees worldwide (20%) say their job impacts their mental health in a negative way, and women seem to have it worse (23% vs. 16% of men). At the end of the workday, 43% of employees are "often" or "always" exhausted, and 78% say that stress negatively impacts their work performance. That stress from*

---

[12] *.Fortune, Bywill Daniels, February 8, 2023*

work carries into our personal lives, too, as employees say work negatively impacts their home life (71%), wellbeing (64%), and relationships (62%).

If leadership is to rise to the challenge of building a corporate culture that enables talent to perform, it appears the shift must be strategic.

If organizations plan to improve employee engagement, there is no better place to start than by identifying the blockers in the culture screen. Asking "what getting in the way of you being all that you could be?" This is a leadership role. Leaders are the key enablers of the workplace conditions.

A final word

While there is a strong emphasis on inclusion and engagement this in no way relieves leaders from the responsibility to make decisions and set direction. Leadership is still critical – but this approach recognizes that effective leadership comes from developing followers rather than being given a title.

A great leader may use different styles. They may inspire. They may be inclusive and engaging. They may be detail focused. They may be action oriented. Whatever their bias they call on ALL these qualities when required. They are wise enough to know that they may not have all the answers, but strong enough to listen to others and make the required decisions.

12 Culture, trust, agility, and innovation

> Culture is the enabler of achieving strategic goals based on how people behave and execute their work. Trust, agility , and innovation are individual and organizational outcomes, that are highly influenced by individual and collective behavior. They don't just happen.

While the title of this short chapter is quite "a mouthful," it addresses one of the foundational organizational outcomes that an effective culture produces. That of being capable of highly competitive levels of innovation, creativity, and agility.

Organizations must have the ability to come up with new ideas and respond fast to rapid changes in customers' needs and wishes. Also, to respond to the changing needs of the marketplace and the economic environment an organization operates within.

Many organizations state that they want to achieve these outcomes and exhort their employees to "make it happen." The challenge is that the way you make it happen is by hiring great talent (of course) and then creating a work environment that ALLOWS it to happen.

Sure, financial incentives and recognition and rewards are important but for many people, who have a natural drive to be creative, they just want to be given the opportunity. A blocked culture screen impairs their ability to make this happen. Eventually people may start to shrug and ask, "what's the point?"

What gets in the way of innovation? In many cases it is fear. Fear of failure – but also fear of repercussions. If the work climate is one of compliance – "follow instructions," then the risk to innovation is being criticized by direct management. This can include being singled out and criticized in front of one's work peers.

This criticism also instills fear from having "stepped out of line" and how this may impact future career prospects. Their performance reviews may say "this person tends not to follow instructions," or "this person takes it on their own to go off and do things without asking."

These types of blockages are strongly linked to culture and the work environment. Bureaucracy. Poor policies and procedures. Lack of supportive leadership.

It may be that an organization has "innovation and creativity" stated as one of its' values, but in many cases when a person exercises personal innovation in their work, they can be criticized. A direct inconsistency between what is said and what is done. People will believe in what is demonstrated by leadership behaviour – not what is said in general statements or announced on a promotional poster on the wall of the workplace.

Sure, there can be the risk of misunderstanding. "You want me to follow procedures, but you want me to innovate? How do these two things work together?" That can be a valid question, which will eventually come back to the agility and speed that a direct manager or supervisor can exercise. Positive responsiveness to people's ideas is a critical reinforcer of the desired behaviors.

Do they have the authority to say, "sounds like a great idea – let's go ahead and try it." Or are they likely to respond "Oh, I don't have the authority to do that. We need to raise a request – or get another department involved or schedule a meeting etc. etc."

Supervisors themselves may also be impacted by the fear of failure in terms of exercising what they think is their authority to manage what happens in their work teams. They may be so focused on "execution of task" that they are fearful that any deviation they authorize to try something new, might result in limitations to their own career. Maybe play it safe and shift the responsibility to someone else to make the decision.

The importance of fear was reinforced by an article in 2022 by McKinsey[13] who had studied the problem and concluded that this was a major factor in slowing down or stopping innovation.

Many organizations adopt knowledge management systems that provide a conduit to collecting, storing, and disseminating ideas that people generate. These capabilities must be paired with solid support that allows the information in these systems to be thoughtfully yet rapidly evaluated, assessed, and converted into value added activity.

Culture provides the environment within which responsiveness to change can thrive. To understand this, the following example of an adapted Lewin change model can be used:

Lewin suggested a three-step change management model – unfreeze, change, and refreeze. The overall cycle time for change to take place is the sum of the three steps. An effective culture reduces the time span of the total change management process.

---

[13] "Fear factor: Overcoming human barriers to innovation" June 3, 2022, https://www.mckinsey.com/capabilities/strategy-and-corporate-finance/our-insights/fear-factor-overcoming-human-barriers-to-innovation

Firstly, trust will exist. People will stop asking "what's behind the change?" "Is this all about layoffs?" "What's the hidden agenda?" The workforce will be more willing to accept that the suggestions and ideas for change are for the benefit of all, and will spend little time on argument, procrastination or second guessing their management and supervision.

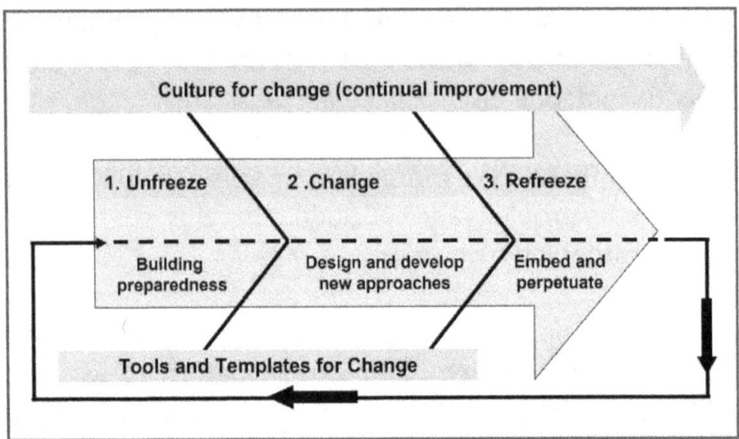

Second, open communication will exist. In all likelihood, there will already be an acceptance that there "could be a better way" and when someone has an idea to change something, others are more likely not to obstruct the suggestions moving forward.

Thirdly, there will be a willingness on the part of management to assess the benefits of the change from not just a "saving money" perspective (which remains important) but also including considerations of other stakeholders. Will customers benefit or is it negative? Will employees benefit or will it make their job harder or excessively complex?

Creating a culture for change will shorten all three phases of the process. Unfreezing will be faster with less disruption. Changing will be faster because people will have already been involved in the practicality of "operationalizing" the new ideas. And the refreezing will be more successful. There will be fewer people continuing to do things the old way.

Organizations often talk about "out of the box" thinking. The challenge is that "why put people in a box in the first place?" If the "box" is "the way that we do business around here" then maybe the culture screen is blocked up already? Maybe the policies and procedures are out of line with the strategic imperative of supporting innovation?

A great summary of the blocks to innovation was published by "teamup" blog[14] titled "How to Remove Innovation Blocks and Encourage Great Ideas." This lists four blocks.

First - sharing insights isn't encouraged. Amazingly the blog suggested that "in an average company, top management is aware only of 4 percent of the organization's problems. Even middle management has knowledge only of mere 9 percent." That is a systemic culture issue.

Second – there is no system for ideas. The blog has a great example of a simple system to capture and share ideas. This is NOT your traditional suggestion box.

Third – poor or missing communication. Again, a culture issue. Can be either simply poor communication OR more importantly and more damaging supervisors or others "stealing" ideas. Once again, the blog provides a great schematic of a simple communication approach on idea status. (It might also be a poor communication style issue as discussed in understanding different personalities)

Lastly – lack of organization. Again, an indicator of misaligned communications OR a failure of "the necessary tools and equipment to do my job." The blog has a great example of what might be applied.

---

[14] https://blog.teamup.com/2022/11/16/remove-innovation-blocks/

Resistance to change is disruptive and can lead to passive / aggressive behaviour. This benefits no one and stands in the way of organizational innovation and creativity "implemented at speed."

Desired outcomes such as agility and innovation are created by the behavior of people and the capability of the "system" within which they work. Is the system "fit for purpose?" Creating an effective culture with few if any blockages to the culture screen is a foundation of these desired outcomes. Hiring talent is only one aspect of achieving the desired goals.

13 Purpose, task, and relationships

> Task is about what an organization does. Relationships are about how they go about doing it. Integration is the effective bringing together both strategically and operationally both task and relationships, to optimize system effectiveness.

Organizational purpose has been touched on several times. It is seen by many as the "new focus" for business. CEOs of the US based Business Round Table issued the following statement in 2019:

> **Business Roundtable today announced the release of a new Statement on the Purpose of a Corporation signed by 181 CEOs who commit to lead their companies for the benefit of all stakeholders – customers, employees, suppliers, communities and shareholders.**

There are mixed feelings about both the value of, and the commitment to, this statement by CEOs, and about their actual performance. We leave these to the reader to research. The key point linked to the critical role of corporate culture is how this statement should change the way the business is run. Re-creating and refreshing "the way we do things around here."

If CEOs really believe that things need to change, making a statement will not make it happen. CHANGING something is what is required. Why not start with building a workplace culture that is "fit for purpose?"

Business has always had a purpose.

Every single organization that has been created has a purpose. The purpose it was created for. In strategy and business planning texts the use of "purpose" has long been established as one of the most important aspects.

Many will have heard about or been involved with "mission, vision, and values," or "mission and purpose." From these are developed business goals and objectives. These are developed based on what the owners and investors of the business want the organization to achieve. Its purpose.

These expectations are "negotiated" with management who has the responsibility to put the system, plans, and actions in place to deliver the desired results. (We know this – theoretically this is what organizational design is about – but does it include a strategic approach to culture?)

An important aspect of achieving employee engagement is ensuring that everyone in the organization knows both the business purpose, together with their own personal role in achieving that purpose.

WE HAVE A PROBLEM
The PURPOSE statement is incomplete.

The message that many employees hear in "for profit" organizations, is that the purpose is heavily driven by making money. Sure, the investor wants to make money – in fact a "for profit" organization MUST make money to survive. But was that the purpose the organization was created for? Is making money the ONLY thing that is important?

If this is true, then everything else that is said about all other stakeholders is deemed to be a secondary priority. Management may not see this as the reality but for many at the front lines, this is the message that they hear.

Culture is not about what an organizations says it is committed to, but about what it demonstrates by the way that it behaves.

Being "purpose driven" requires a governance framework that places equal importance on both its' business purpose and its' social purpose.

- **Business purpose** – what we are in business to do. The purpose for which we were created in terms of the value we create for society through the products and services we provide.
- **Social purpose** – the way we behave while we pursue our business purpose. How we act as a responsible member of society or societies within which we operate.

The reason this is a governance issue is because it must start with being a stated and practiced framework for how the business is to be operated. It is strategic by nature. This goes beyond legal compliance and embraces behaving responsibly.

In much the same way as society expects individuals to behave responsibly, so it expects a business to do the same. This challenge has grown in importance and complexity. When businesses were predominantly national in nature, they behaved within the society within which they operated.

PURPOSE

How does this organization add value to society?

BUSINESS PURPOSE	**SOCIAL PURPOSE**
Products & services that are created	**Impacts on stakeholders**
TASK ASPECTS	**RELATIONSHIPS**

Now many organizations are supra-national, operating in many societies. Each country or society would expect them to behave as a responsible individual within their own, local society. While this means working within the laws and regulations of each society, how is the required behavior defined?

Business – both for profit and not-for-profit have achieved maturity in focusing on their business purpose. This can be considered the task of getting the job done. Focusing on the outcomes related to the products and services that are produced. Note that making a profit is a stakeholder outcome for investors. This is done by effective task execution.

Social purpose is NOT the amount of charitable giving that takes place, or the number of hours that employees are "given time off work to perform charitable activities." Social Purpose is described well by a non-profit, which is part of the United Way in British Columbia, Canada. Their website states"

Social Purpose is a fast-emerging business driver - a holistic approach to business in which a company defines its reason for being the way in which it creates value - both for business and society. It helps grow the business, creates resiliency, and strengthens the work the company does and the context in which it operates. Social Purpose is good for business and good for society.

Governance ensures a Purpose led organization.

Corporate governance is the framework of rules, practices, structures, and processes through which an organization is directed and managed. A company's board of directors is often the primary force influencing corporate governance.

However, in a private company it may be a board of advisors or the owner themselves. These people set "the tone at the top." This is the foundation of a purpose driven organization. (This is why the "G" in ESG is so critical). These people decide how the business will be operated.

In the graphic below, those in a governance role determine both the business purpose and the social purpose. What is to be done (the task) and how it is to be done (the relationships).

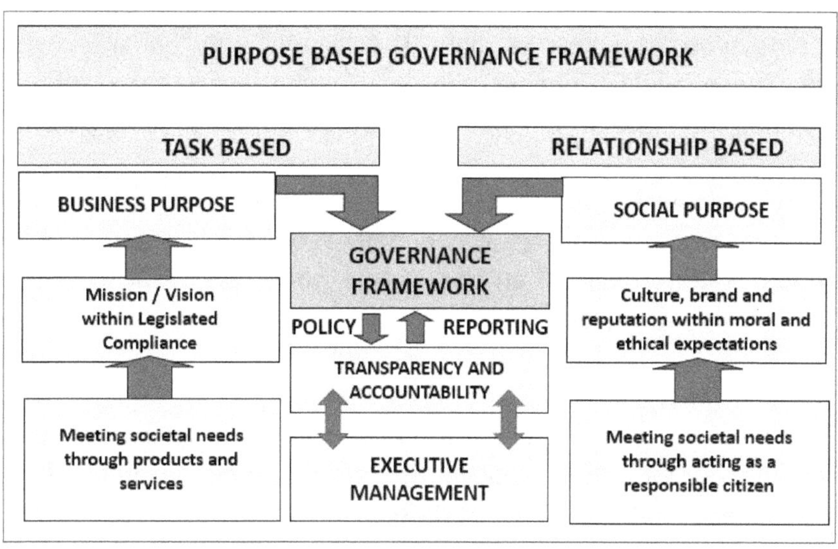

Directing and managing "the task"

Managing tasks have always been a high priority because that is the primary reason organizations are established. To take a market need or a great idea or innovation and scale it up to create a commercially viable enterprise. That is what investors like to see. They want to put their money into something that has a need and can make money.

Applying "science" to managing tasks has also developed over the years – in fact the industrial revolution was at the heart of doing just that. As techniques like mass production evolved experts like Alfred Sloan, and Frederick Taylor analyzed and enhanced the way work was performed.

Many of their approaches were then used when the Japanese started re-building their industry after World War 2 when they visited US manufacturers like Ford.

The Japanese built upon this base and significantly enhanced task management through approaches such as TPS (Toyota Production System). In particular approaches developed by J Edwards Deming, an American engineer and statistician, were also applied to use statistical sampling to further develop "the task" activity, that significantly enhanced product quality. These quality management approaches were then adopted by other global manufacturers. The management of task became a key focus.

During this refinement of task, it became evident that the involvement and engagement of the workforce was equally required. Processes could only be effectively improved when the people doing the work were actively involved in suggesting ideas and innovations.

This brought in the era of TQM or Total Quality Management. This also ushered in the era of "excellence award schemes." These awards were presented to organizations that had adopted compliance with a rigorous integrated and holistic framework that included all stakeholders and resources.

Various "models for excellence" were created. Common to all of these was the involvement and engagement of the workforce. Some organizations were successful in applying these ideas and reaping a significant competitive advantage.

Some of these organizations adopted a strategic approach to planning and execution, such as the Hoshin Kanri model. But the question remains, have people and the human aspects of business yet reached the strategic importance of process management?

Directing and managing relationships.

The simple answer is no – not yet. Granted a few organizations have reinvented their approach to strategy but many continue to focus on task. Building strategies, plans and actions around the process aspects of achieving the desired outputs and outcomes.

The following table was instrumental in focusing attention on the predictability of defects or unplanned process results when planning and managing the task aspects of work.

SIGMA level	Defects per million (transaction, units)	Defect Percent	Rating	Financial impact
2	308,537	30.8537%	Non-competitive	Unknown
3	66,807	6.6807%		25 – 40% of sales
4	6,210	0.6210%	Industry average	15 – 25% of sales
5	233	0.0233%		5 – 15% of sales
6	3.4	0.0003%	World class	< 1% of sales

Statistical analysis had revealed that most organizations operated with a process capability of between 3 and 4 Sigma (to keep it simple this is a measure of the number of unplanned variations that can occur).

This meant that for every task, activity, or process, between 6,210 and 66,807 errors would occur for every million operations. The lower number (4 Sigma – industry average at the time) sounds good, right? After all that is only 0.62% defects or 99.38% results that meet requirements – items that are meeting expectations.

What attracted attention was that at this (4 Sigma) level of errors or mistakes, the wasted cost was between 15% and 40% of sales. That is an immense number. It appeared that no other opportunity existed to save as much money as to invest in process improvement. As an example, over a period of five years GE spent over $1 billion on training people in an approach called 6 Sigma aimed at reducing errors, by improving process predictability and performance so that variation was reduced to 6 Sigma.

In the early stages the company calculated that it was saving almost that amount of money per year through process improvement. How about if this approach were applied to the predictability of human behavior?

SIGMA level	Errors in human judgment	Defect Percent	Rating	Financial impact
2	308,537	30.8537%	Non-competitive	Unknown
3	66,807	6.6807%		25 – 40% of sales
4	6,210	0.6210%	Industry average	15 – 25% of sales
5	233	0.0233%		5 – 15% of sales
6	3.4	0.0003%	World class	< 1% of sales

By changing just one column – process errors to errors in human judgement, a similar impact can be seen. How predictable is human behavior in an organization? To what degree are people recruited, trained, supervised, and developed so that there is some level of predictability in their behavior?

"Moments of truth" is a phrase that was developed by Jan Carlson when he was CEO of SAS at a time when the company was focusing on the human aspects of customer service. As Carlson stated *"every time that there is an interaction between one of our employees and a member of the public, this is a moment of truth. That interaction will determine in the public's mind, what it is that our company believes in and how we behave."*

Moments of truth occur all the time in the workplace. When people talk to each other. When managers talk to staff. When a "line manager" seeks support from another work area. When a customer has a problem. When a supplier needs help. When third parties talk to staff. There is probably a greater opportunity for variation in relationships than processes!

CULTURE IS ABOUT MOMENTS OF TRUTH

Every time there is a human interaction, it will be the determinant of the organizations real culture. How relationships work, is how the culture operates.

The only way to enhance the predictability of human behavior is to create a climate where expectations are clearly defined, and leaders reinforce expectations both by how they behave as well as how they deal with unplanned behavioral situations.

This starts with effective governance defining what sort of behavior is expected to underpin the creation and sustaining of critical relationships. A great culture is all about sustaining positive, effective relationships between and among stakeholders whose collaborative efforts are critical to success of the business model.

- Relationships between departments
- Relationships with suppliers and other partners
- Relationships with customers and clients
- Relationships among members of the workforce
- Relationship between executive leadership

All these relationships enable the execution of work. This can only happen where there is a statement of organizational values. These values "about how people are expected to behave" are central to creating agreements such as a Code of Conduct or Code of Ethics.

Once again there must be broad-based acceptance of behavioral expectations. It cannot be imposed by management, but management, after receiving input and assessing the cultural reality of the society that they operate in, must provide clear expectations.

OPERATING UNDER CONTROLLED CONDITIONS

Avoid surprises by determining what controlled conditions are expected to be.

Organizations usually know what controlled conditions mean. These are often included in policies and procedures. But these usually focus on the control of processes. Are all the people operating under controlled conditions in terms of their behavior? Are they expected to effectively communicate? To collaborate and cooperate with others? To care about one another's well-being?

Only through this attention to culture and relationship management through effective leadership, will the culture screen be free of problems and impediments. How we behave as responsible individuals and responsible members of society is equally important to how we get the job done. Culture doesn't evolve but is managed strategically.

14 Psychology in the workplace.

My job as a manager would be easy - if it wasn't for the people problems.

This is a familiar comment often made by managers who have to deal with "people issues." Too often people's issues are seen as an HR problem to be resolved – but in many cases the responsibility rests with the immediate supervisor. But as we discussed, time is the problem. People "are a challenge."

Yet it is "all about people." Managers as leaders play a critical role in ensuring a "clean and clear" culture screen. What skills and tools do leaders need to help with this?

There has been much study on the application of psychology in the business environment. However there remains much skepticism towards investing time and effort in broadly developing such knowledge. Yet "understanding people" is increasingly a key success factor for anyone in a management position.

Understanding people – who they are, why they behave the way that they do, is an important foundation of building an effective culture. While psychology has been around as a profession for a long time, it is becoming more valuable as organizations seek to create work environments that engage people.

This is way beyond studies in motivation for pay and compensation purposes, or about understanding "types" of people who "fit in."

The reality is that people are individuals. Unique. While they have certain traits and tendencies each one is a unique "package." Everyone not only has their own unique personality, but they have been molded by the cumulative effects of their life experiences. The American Psychological Association states the case well:

> Psychology is critical to the workplace. It helps managers at all levels of organizations select, support, motivate and train employees. It also helps businesses design products, build better workspaces and foster healthy behavior.
>
> Through their scientific research, psychologists are discovering new ways to increase productivity, identify training and development needs, and implement policies proven to attract and retain the best employees. By studying how people interact with technology and equipment, psychologists can help make these tools more user-friendly and prevent errors, whether we are using everyday products or life-critical technologies.
>
> *American Psychological Association*

There are three critical areas where the application of psychological knowledge is becoming more important. Hiring and selection, individual and team development, and relationship development. The use of these tools requires investment – and the challenge is often budget limitations. But there is a way to assess the ROI on this, and many other investments related to enhanced workforce development.

Creating the ROI of culture

As discussed earlier, it was only when organizations started to realize the real cost of quality failures that it awoke to the value of investing to stop these failures happening. The same is true of the cost of poor culture. Most of the costs are hidden so that management is not aware of the opportunity that can come from investing additional funds in the "people" side of the business.

THE COSTS OF CULTURE			
Prevention	**Appraisal**	**Failure**	
		Internal failure	External failure

The costs of culture are of three types. Each of these must be fully known and understood. Only by understanding the excess costs (failures) that are being incurred can investments be justified that eliminate or reduce the root causes.

Prevention	Investments to create a positive culture. To eliminate problems and issues related to people.
Appraisal	Checks and assessments to sustain a positive culture with both existing and new members of the workforce.
Internal failures	Internal problems and issues that occur internally within the organization, that incur added resources.
External failures	Problems that occur externally to the organization caused by a negative culture, including problems that are not recognized.

The two "failures" categories are those costs that make up the bulk of the hidden costs of poor culture. In the 6 Sigma example earlier, these can be between 15% and 40% of operating costs. If these are not being captured, then creating an ROI on prevention costs is impossible.

More detail on the costs of poor culture is provided in the book of the same title. As far as failure costs are concerned, they come in three types.

- Financial surprises. When people take unexpected action that incur unplanned costs. (Acting illegally, missing deadlines).
- Buried costs. The amount of costs that are currently being incurred but that could be eliminated if there were no barriers to an effective culture. (Those excess operating costs caused by the culture screen stopping talent from optimum performance).
- Lost opportunities. The potential for financial savings and growth opportunities that will come from a workforce that is fully engaged.

The first question then in spending funds for psychological tools is to ask, "what problem are we trying to solve?" Reflecting back to the impacts already discussed (but possible not being measured financially) include:

- Cost of turnover (hiring, retraining, work impact).
- Demotions, or terminations
- Excessive absenteeism and other leave.
- Higher client turnover, caused by poor relationships, especially human interaction.
- Loss of key suppliers if staff are "too hard to work with."
- Loss of supplier's willingness to share ideas for fear of the client "stealing" them.
- Greater regulatory interventions and attention due to being classified as a "problem organization."
- Higher audit fees due to assessment of a poor "tone at the top" (see concepts of CoSo framework application).
- Legal costs and disputes (fines, penalties, supplier disputes, mediation / arbitration).
- Impact of delays to plans and schedules caused by lack of communication, collaboration, and cooperation.

- Operational cost impacts due to poor tools, equipment, systems.
- Impact of poor leadership – problem escalation, HR, or senior management involvement.

These are just a few. So how can the application of psychological knowledge and skills be applied to mitigate some of these? Investments here would be in either prevention costs or appraisal – as they are investments to reduce or eliminate unplanned failures elsewhere.

Hiring and selection

The use of psychological assessments has been used for some time as part of the hiring process. For senior executives this has often included a "battery" of tests aimed at really understanding what drives and motivates an individual and identifying their underlying strengths.

The goal of using any sort of psychological evaluations at the time of hire is to increase the probability of a "good hire." That is potential underlying personality attributes that might impact performance in the workplace can be identified. With current laws on privacy, making it increasingly challenging to obtain accurate references for potential employees, the application of other approaches is becoming more important.

This is way beyond "typing" of a person to ensure they are a good "fit" for the business. Again, every person is unique and at time of hire this uniqueness needs to be understood as well as possible. The three main reasons are to assess:

- The individuals' attitudes, values, and beliefs compared to the organization's values, that have been developed to guide personal behavior in "the way we do things around here."
- To understand the individuals' strengths and capabilities so as to best work with them to apply both their current skills, education, and experience as well as their underlying potential, for their own

growth and benefit and for the organization, starting with their immediate work team.
- To create the "needs analysis" for the individuals personal development plan in both the short term (onboarding / orientation), and longer term – their personal development plan. This includes identifying potential behavioral "blind spots" where awareness will be important.

Using these approaches at hiring provides no guarantees of success. However, given the challenge of knowing enough about an individual at the time of hire, using well thought through and structured assessment tools can increase the probability of success. Both for the organization and the individual.

Individual and team development

Psychological assessment approaches have also been used extensively in "team building" and individual development. If a psychological assessment tool has been used at hiring this will already provide a foundation for individual development.

The concept of work teams developed significantly during the quality management era, when "task collaboration" was recognized as being important. It has also been used during development sessions of senior leadership teams, sometimes including Boards.

Personal development, related to working with others must start with "knowing self." This is the first "stepping-stone" in understanding how team dynamics are impacted by the unique personalities of each team member. While this information may have been developed with an individual at the time of hiring, it is important that it be shared in the initial stages of any group development activity. It helps people understand each other and how to interact more effectively.

There are several goals of using psychological tools to enhance group development that may include:

- Helping each person understand their own unique personality and style, so as to understand "how others see and hear them."
- Understand how each person has a unique style of giving and receiving communications from others and how understanding this will improve interactions and information sharing.
- To understand the difference in personalities among team members and how these differences affect several areas of personal interaction.
- To understand the possible gap between who a person "really is" and how others may see them at work, because they don't always express their real personality, values, and feelings.
- To understand peoples' needs in the workplace to be themselves and free up areas of talent that may be suppressed.
- To identify the strengths of individuals in a group and how collaboration can allow these strengths to flourish.
- To build acceptance and respect for differences between people rather than seeing these as barriers.

Work teams usually work in constant close relationships with each other – such as executive leadership teams. Unless they can come together and operate with a "constancy of purpose" there is a danger that cooperation and collaboration will not adequately develop and might be replaced by protective silos that will impact the operation of the whole organization.

There are a number of challenges in applying these tools for team development – in addition to the cost already cited. Time can be a problem – and that is why the development of behavioral strategy must be the highest-level priority. The development of people is not an "add on" to business where the success rate is measured in the number of hours of training that is being provided.

Team development is also often thought of as linear – and event that people attend and "once its' done, its' over." This is dangerous. The dynamics of team effectiveness is a continuing process. Team members change and that can change the whole dynamic of the group. (This is one reason why shared values are so critical, in that they perpetuate a consistent approach to how things are done).

People also change and develop, both as individuals as well as in their understanding of the workplace and its challenges and in the dynamics of working with others. Thus, some continuity must be applied to sustain ongoing development.

Finally, it is unwise to try and "ride many horses in the same race." This means that there are many different tools out there in the marketplace, that all have unique approaches and language associated with them. Using a variety of different tools – either for different aspects of human development, or at different times can bring confusion and inconsistency.

It is recommended that a "preferred supplier" be adopted, or as a minimum a supplier who uses the same tools and approach. In this way, as the development tools become more broadly used the language becomes familiar so that understanding among people is enhanced.

Relationship development

This aspect of applying psychological tools to help with understanding people and human relationships may seem similar to the previous section. The opportunity is that it has not been widely accepted yet.

There are two areas for emphasis. First is leadership development. While we discussed work teams above – which would usually include the leader of the work team, assessment tools and subsequent development based on an understanding of self MUST become a mandatory requirement of ALL people in management positions.

Cross functional collaboration and cooperation has become critical for an effective and high functioning business model. This requires that every manager has the skills to enable this capability starting with their own responsibility to "set an example."

Many organizations use evaluation tools such as the 360° assessment. This is often a core aspect for manager evaluation. One of the problems with using these tools is that many are based on generic question sets. To be effective, the questions should be based on expected behaviors that the organization itself has stated in documents such as its code of ethics or conduct or its corporate values.

Leadership development should ensure that these foundations for behavior that have been agreed, form the basis of the assessment approaches. These assessments for a critical part of the strategic management of culture in that the results provide the "check" aspects of the plan, do, check, and act business model.

The second, often overlooked aspect of relationship development is building relationships with business partners other than the workforce. Today's business model sees collaboration as a key aspect when working with customers, suppliers, community, regulators and others.

Where these relationships are considered strategically critical, joint development sessions should take place during which tools to help mutual understanding are used. The approach would be very similar to the team building approach but would extend externally from the organization. While this may create complications related to the approaches used, these challenges can usually be dealt with through discussion and looking for "best fit" approaches.

One aspect of extending this approach to external partners is that it will quickly reveal whether there are underlying conflicts of values between business partners. While some degree of this is inevitable, working with partners who do not share an organizations values has the potential for problems and issues "down the road."

As a final note on these relationship development approaches, the evolving need and obligation for organizations to include areas like climate change and emission in their (level 3) environmental reporting are going to make it critical that a high degree of collaboration is achieved. Working in collaboration with others has never been as important as it is in the current reality.

15 Love – a final word

In a radio interview that followed publication of the book I wrote with Dr. Peter Smyth of leadership[15], we were asked what was one of the most important qualities that a leader requires. After a pause, Peter replied, "well, essentially it starts with love. You need to love people." There was a stunned silence, and then Peter went on to explain.

The key to his explanation is that love results in tolerance, respect, understanding, empathy, and a number of qualities that can only come from a level of attachment or concern for others. A great leader must "care" about people. In spite of, or maybe even because of the unique and challenging nature of human personalities, unless a leader starts out by "loving" the people that work for him or her, it will be hard to deliver on the desired behaviors.

LOVE CAN BE DESCRIBED AS:

- **strong affection for another arising out of kinship or personal ties;**
- **affection based on admiration, benevolence, or common interests;**
- **the object of attachment, devotion, or admiration;**
- **unselfish loyal and benevolent concern for the good of another.**

Managing and leading people means understanding and accepting the fickle and often unpredictable nature of human behavior. A great leader balances the importance of task with building relationships.

[15] Shepherd, Nick., Smyth, Peter. (2012), "Reflective Leaders and High-performance organizations," iUniverse.

Many leaders may find this ridiculous. Generations of leaders have seen their positions as separate and distinct from those of the workforce. There is "no time" to deal with that level of detail. This is especially true when an organizational grows to achieve "scale."

When the workforce numbers in the thousands the "easy" route is to manage people like any other resource – as a coherent and predictable commodity that can be managed, controlled, and directed as though it was a generic group.

This reality to change the relations with and between people was predicted in "The Centerless Corporation." Chapter three of the book is titled "The triumph of people power" and included discussion on the changing relationships and emergence of a new partnership between "a corporation and its' employees." This is not new!

Certain organizations have been able to treat people as humans. To exhibit the behaviors that underpin a caring approach. To recognize that if you REALLY care about the people who turn your strategies, plans and actions into reality you focus on the culture you create.

CRITICAL STEPS TO BUILDING AN EFFECTIVE CULTURE

Governance – set people centric policies and procedures that show you care.
Integrate – ensure people are actively engaged operational decisions
Leadership – ensure leaders reflect the commitment to caring about people
But most of all....

SHOW THAT YOU CARE - EVERYWHERE

How does this happen? Policies, and procedures must align everywhere to the commitment to "enabling" people to perform. Leadership everywhere must be as well trained and empowered in their interpersonal knowledge and understanding as they are in management of tasks.

All areas of assessment, measurement, and performance feedback must include ensuring the task is being achieved and that the desired culture is being sustained. This is NOT an HR role. It is a strategic, total organizational commitment.

While each of us can strive to love what we do, it may be equally important to strive to love those who share the journey with us.

16 Call to action

Hopefully several aspects of this book find some resonance with the reader. The challenge we all face is making the world a better place for those who follow us. We also need to make today's world a better place, in particular renew the way that business operates.

The goal of the book is to help identify where problems are and encourage those in leadership positions to take a step back and ask whether the workplace could be in better condition. The best way to do that is to get people involved.

If people can be encouraged to speak up and speak out, they will be more fulfilled. Yet each of us, wherever we work, must take personal responsibility for what we do and how we act.

One phrase that was in one of my clients values many years ago was "to encourage and support constructive dissonance." Speak up when you see a problem or opportunity – but don't just complain. Suggest what needs to be done. Let your voice be heard but recognize that there may be facts, issues, and concerns that you are not aware of.

Those in a leadership position have an advantage – they can act and influence change. But so can anyone be an influencer. I like the trim tab analogy, that was originally identified by Buckminster Fuller and is often as a metaphor for leadership and personal empowerment; (originally published in the February 1972 issue of Playboy). He said:

> *Something hit me very hard once, thinking about what one little man could do. Think of the Queen Mary—the whole ship goes by and then comes the rudder. And there's a tiny thing at the edge of the rudder called a trim tab.*
>
> *It's a miniature rudder. Just moving the little trim tab builds a low pressure that pulls the rudder around. Takes almost no effort at all. So, I said that the little individual can be a trim tab. Society thinks it's going right by you, that it's left you altogether. But if you're doing dynamic things mentally, the fact is that you can just put your foot out like that and the whole big ship of state is going to go.*

In 2019 it was referred to by Jeff Bridges in his Cecil B. DeMille Award acceptance speech at the 76th Golden Globes:

> *Bucky made the analogy that a trim tab is an example of how the individual is connected to society and how we affect society. And I like to think of myself as a trim tab. All of us are trim tabs. We might seem like we're not up to the task, but we are, man. We're alive! We can make a difference! We can turn this ship in the way we wanna go, man!*

As individuals this is what we can strive to be – a trim tab. An influencer. No matter what level in the organization. Even the CEO needs to influence the board.

It all starts with belief in the ability of each of us to make a difference. Even if we start by looking at our own behavior and attitude towards others. Making sure we don't complain without offering solutions. Not criticize others. Give people the benefit of the doubt. Don't gossip or spread rumors.

Central to it all is caring. Both about ourselves and about others. Caring about how our actions affect others. Caring about how responsibly we act.

If each of us cares and acts responsibly, we can build the foundations for a better future.

17 Bibliography

Becker, Brian. E., Huselid, Mark. A., Ulrich, F. Dave. The HR Scorecard," 2001, Harvard Business Press.

Blanchard, Ken, and O'Connor, Michael (1997) *Managing by Values*, Berrett-Koehler.

Buckingham, M., Coffman, C., (1999), *First break all the rules; what the world's greatest managers do differently*, Simon & Schuster

Campanella, Jack (1999) *Principles of Quality Costs, 3rd edition*, Quality Press, ASQ.

Charas, S., Lupushor, (2022), *Humanizing Human Capital,* Matt Holly division of BenBella Books

Cohen, Ben, and Warwick, Mal (2006) *Values Driven Business*, Berrett-Koehler.

Covey, Stephen, M. R. (2018), *The Speed of Trust (This changes everything),* Free Press

Covey, Stephen. R., (1990), *Principle-Centered Leadership*, Summit Books

Crosby, Phil (1979) *Quality is Free*, Signet.

Edvinsson, L., and Malone. M. S. (1997) *Intellectual Capital*, pp.168–169, Harper Business.

Fitz-enz, Jac (2000) *The ROI of Human Capital*, AMACOM.

Galloway, S. (2017), *The Four, The hidden DNA of Amazon, Apple, Facebook, and Google*, Portfolio / Penguin

Gleeson-White, Jane (2014) *Six Capitals: The Revolution Capitalism has to have – or can accountants save the planet*, Allen & Unwin.

Hood, Daniel (2019) *Trust is just the beginning*, Accounting Today (Study from ACCA, IFAC, and CA ANZ), March 4.

IFAC (2015) *Materiality in Integrated Reporting*, Integrated Reporting <IR> and International Federation of Accountants.

IIRC (2013) *The International <IR> Framework*, International Integrated Reporting Council, December.

Lev, Baruch, and Gu, Feng (2016) *The End of Accounting*, Wiley.

Johnson, Thomas. H., and Kaplan, Robert, S. (1987) *Relevance Lost: The Rise and Fall of Management Accounting*, Harvard Business School Press.

Kaplan, Robert. S., and Norton, David. P. (1996) *The Balanced Scorecard*, Harvard Business Review Press.

Kaplan, Robert. S., and Norton, David. P. (2006) *Alignment*, Harvard Business School Publishing.

Kearns. P., and Woollard, Stuart (2019) *The Mature Corporation*, Cambridge Scholars Press.

Liker, Jeffrey. K. (2011) *Toyota Under Fire: How Toyota faced the challenges of the recall and came out stronger*, McGraw Hill.

Liker, Jeffrey. K. (2004) *The Toyota Way*, McGraw Hill.

Liker, Jeffrey. K., and Hoseus, Michael (2008) *Toyota Culture: The Heart and Soul of the Toyota Way*, McGraw Hill.

Liker, Jeffrey. K., and Meier, David. P. (2007) *Toyota Talent; Developing Your People the Toyota Way*, McGraw Hill.

Magee, David (2007) *How Toyota Became #1*, Portfolio.

Nayar, Vineet (2010) *Employees First, Customers Second*, Harvard Business Press.

Pasternack, Bruce, A., & Viscio, Albert. J., (1998) *The centerless corporation*, Simon & Schuster

Peters, Sandra (2020) *FASB Turns Up the Heat on Goodwill Impairment Testing*, CFA Institute, February 12.

Rother, Mike (2010) *Toyota Kata*, McGraw Hill.

Schmidt, Eric., and Rosenberg, Jonathan (2014) *How Google Works*, Hachette Book Group Ltd.

Shepherd, N. (2005) *Governance, Accountability and Sustainable Development: An agenda for the 21st century*, Thomson Carswell, Canada.

Shepherd, N., and Adams, M. (2014) *Unrecognized Intangible Assets: Identification, Management and Reporting*, Statements in

Management Accounting series, Institute of Management Accountants.

Shepherd, N. (2021) *How Accountants Lost their Balance*, Kindle Direct Publishing (Eduvision / Jannas Publications).

Shepherd, N. (2021) *Corporate Culture – Combining Purpose and Values*, Kindle Direct Publishing (Eduvision / Jannas Publications).

Smyth, Peter, and Shepherd. N. (2012) *Reflective Leaders and High-Performance Organizations*, iUniverse Publishing.

Stewart, T. (1997) *Intellectual Capital: The New Wealth of organizations*, pp. 232–233, Doubleday.

Stewart, Tom (1997) *Intellectual Capital: The New Wealth of Nations*, Currency Doubleday.

Wallis, Jim (2010) *Rediscovering Values*, Simon & Schuster.

Weiss, David. S. (2000) *High Performance HR – Leveraging Human Resources for Competitive Advantage*, John Wiley.

Nick (A) Shepherd
Author

Experienced business professional, thinker, author, and futurist
FRSA., FCPA., FCGA., FCCA., FCMC

Nick has over 50 years of varied work experience including senior general management and finance roles. From 1989 to 2018 he was active in his own management consulting and professional development company.

Currently he still spends time on research and writing, that focuses in the areas of organizational sustainability, human capital, and integrated reporting. Nick has experience working in, and with private family business, public corporations, and governments and NPO's, both in Canada and internationally.

Since his (semi) retirement in late 2017 Nick has added to his books and focused on organizational culture, including a focus on Responsible business.

Nick lives with his wife at an old 1923 log cabin, west of Ottawa, Ontario that sits close to the Ottawa river.

Contact Nick at nick@eduvision.ca
nick@eduvisioninc.co.uk

www.ingramcontent.com/pod-product-compliance
Lightning Source LLC
LaVergne TN
LVHW010107170826
845678LV00012B/2277

9781778130977